D1048701

MARTIN LUTHER KING, JR.
THE LAST INTERVIEW
and OTHER CONVERSATIONS

MELVILLE HOUSE
BROOKLYN · LONDON

MARTIN LUTHER KING, JR.: THE LAST INTERVIEW AND OTHER CONVERSATIONS

Copyright © 2017 by Melville House Publishing

First Melville House printing: January 2017

"'The New Negro'" is reproduced with permission of Elaine Heffner. Originally broadcast on *The Open Mind* on February 10, 1957.

"'Advice for Living'": Courtesy Ebony Media Operations, LLC. All rights reserved. Originally published in *Ebony*, May 1958, p. 112.

"Does Segregation Equal Integration?" is reproduced with permission of Pauline P. Dora. Originally published in abridged form in the *New York Post*, July 11, 1958.

"From *Who Speaks for the Negro?*": Copyright © 1965 by Robert Penn Warren.

"Conversation with Martin Luther King": Copyright © 1968 by The Rabbinical Assembly. Originally published in *Conservative Judaism*, March 25, 1968, vol. 22, no. 3, pp. 1–19.

Melville House Publishing

46 John Street   and

Brooklyn, NY 11201

8 Blackstock Mews

Islington

London N4 2BT

mhpbooks.com   facebook.com/mhpbooks   @melvillehouse

Printed in the United States of America

1   3   5   7   9   10   8   6   4   2

A catalog record for this book is available from the Library of Congress

CONTENTS

v   EDITOR'S NOTE

1   "The New Negro"
Interview with Judge Julius Waties Waring and
Martin Luther King, Jr., by Richard Heffner
PBS, *The Open Mind*
February 10, 1957

15   "Advice for Living"
Ebony
May 1958

23   Does Segregation Equal Integration?
Interview with Mike Wallace
Previously unpublished
June 25, 1958

43   From *Who Speaks for the Negro?*
Interview with Robert Penn Warren
March 18, 1964

85   Conversation with Martin Luther King
68th Annual Convention of the
Rabbinical Assembly
March 25, 1968

EDITOR'S NOTE

We remember the Rev. Dr. Martin Luther King, Jr., as a master rhetorician—perhaps the century's most inspiring. Captivating in person, as in his "I Have a Dream" speech, and commanding on the page, as in the "Letter from a Birmingham Jail," he was a force, eminently and permanently quotable.

It can be startling, then, to imagine him lowered to the rank of mere conversationalist or humble interview subject. What would it be like to speak *with* him? Could he improvise? One might expect to find in this collection some rambling digressions, some overlong pauses, some stuttering, some half-considered ideas. King is, after all, addressing some of the most important questions mankind has ever faced. But there just aren't many of these conversational imperfections to be found.

Instead, as we see again and again in this collection how King's responses to the most daunting questions seem to arrive fully formed, speechlike in their gravity, but natural and rhythmic in their delivery.

This is already apparent in the first piece included here— his first televised talk-show appearance. There, on *The Open Mind* with Richard Heffner, King describes a mass awakening, a new state of black consciousness necessary for revolution. It is sharp cultural criticism and stirring call to action in measured amounts, and yet it feels conversational.

The second selection here is a fascinating piece of publishing history: an installment from King's monthly personal advice column in *Ebony*, which he began in 1957 and discontinued at the end of 1958 on doctor's orders to rest after being stabbed (by a mentally ill woman at a Harlem book signing). In it he answers questions about relationships, white allyship, damaging representations of black characters in children's stories, and more. In advising how a stepfather and his new stepdaughter might overcome their dislike of each other, he explains, in the same terms he conceived of racial integration, that communication between the two parties would surmount their fear of the unknown and bring them together. Indeed, a major takeaway from this collection is that, for King, the political was always personal, and the other way around.

In a long, thoughtful interview with legendary *60 Minutes* journalist Mike Wallace, King draws a distinction between desegregation and integration, pointing out that the latter involves a personal and emotional element that is beyond the politics of desegregation. Unable to have King as a guest on the television show he did before *60 Minutes*, *Night Beat*, Wallace conducted this long interview separately, and published a small portion of it in the *New York Post*. The version included here is the full interview as found in Wallace's papers after his death and has never before been published in its entirety.

The fourth selection comes from the Pulitzer Prize–winning poet and novelist Robert Penn Warren's collection of interviews with civil rights leaders, titled *Who Speaks for the Negro?* Warren's excellently chosen questions make for one of the finest documents we have on King's thoughts on his place in history and the aims of the civil rights movement as a whole.

The last interview here, and the last full interview of King's life, took place at a resort in New York's Catskill Mountains, just ten days before his death. Of course, no one knew that the event, the 68th Annual Convention of the Rabbinical Assembly, would be one of his last. But the resulting transcript—covering subjects as diverse as Black Power as a concept, peace in the Middle East, presidential candidates, Vietnam protests, and the ultimate goal of social justice—provides a fitting close to this collection.

These conversations span a little more than a decade, from 1957 to 1968, encompassing the relatively short time King was in the public eye. Note that among them, he is often asked "What does the future hold?" The question has a tragic ring to it today. But in his inspiring responses we may find a blueprint for today.

"THE NEW NEGRO"

INTERVIEW WITH JUDGE JULIUS WATIES WARING AND
MARTIN LUTHER KING, JR., BY RICHARD HEFFNER
PBS, *THE OPEN MIND*
FEBRUARY 10, 1957

HEFFNER: Well, gentlemen, suppose we begin this discussion by letting me, well, first ask you, Dr. King, in your estimation, what and who is this new Negro?

KING: I think I could best answer that question by saying first that the new Negro is a person with a new sense of dignity and destiny with a new self-respect; along with that is this lack of fear which once characterized the Negro, this willingness to stand up courageously for what he feels is just and what he feels he deserves on the basis of the laws of the land. I think also included would be this self-assertive attitude that you just mentioned. And all of these factors come together to make what seems to me to be the new Negro. I think also I would like to mention this growing honesty which characterizes the Negro today. There was a time that the Negro used duplicity, deception to—rather as a survival technique; although he didn't particularly like conditions he . . . he said he liked them because he felt that the boss wanted to hear that. But now from the housetops, from the kitchens, from the classrooms, and from the pulpit, the Negro says in no uncertain terms that he doesn't like the way he's being treated. So at long last the Negro is telling the truth. And I think this is also one of the basic characteristics of the new Negro.

HEFFNER: Judge Waring, does this sound like an adequate description of the Negro whom you know today?

WARING: Mr. Heffner, I think it's excellent; it's an excellent summary. My observation of the Negro, and I'm speaking in generalities, of course, has been that up to recently he has been a half-man, or a part-man, and now, at last, he is waking up to the fact that he's a whole man, that he's an American citizen, and that he is entitled to rights, no more, no less, than just the ordinary run of the mill American citizen. He's never had that before; he hasn't been allowed to have it. He's been under political domination; he's been under stress; he's been under economic deprivation; he's been a servant, formerly a slave; and now suddenly I see the idea has come to him that he's really, truly a man that can stand up on his own hind legs and tell the truth, and say: "I want not any special privilege; I don't want any special handout; I don't want to be given anything, because the giving idea is all wrong. But I want a chance to become a full man and do my part, be it little or be it big, in the community of our country."

HEFFNER: Doesn't this raise the question of tactics, though? You say, you use the word "honesty," you feel that honesty is important here too. But as a matter of securing for the Negro his rights, do you feel that this aggressiveness, this self-assertiveness will get him more in the long run than going along with contemporary opinion and biding his time, taking it step-by-step as he goes?

KING: I think, I think it's better to be aggressive at this point. It seems to me that it is both historically and sociologically true that privileged classes do not give up their privileges voluntarily. And they do not give them up without strong resistance. And all of the gains that have been made, that we have received in the area of civil rights, have come about because the Negro stood up courageously for these rights, and he was willing to aggressively press on. So I would think that it would be much better in the long run to stand up and be aggressive with understanding goodwill and a sense of discipline, yet things like these should not be substitutes for pressing on. And with this aggressive attitude I believe that we will bring the gains of our civil rights into being much sooner than we would just standing idly by, waiting for these things to be given voluntarily.

HEFFNER: What about the ill will that's generated by the aggressiveness? Certainly your own experience in Montgomery; you've been the target of bomb attacks; you've been the target of verbal and other kinds of violence. How about the ill will that is generated by aggressiveness?

KING: Well, I think that is a necessary phase of the transition. Whenever oppressed people stand up for their rights and rise up against the oppressors, so to speak, the initial response of the oppressor is bitterness. That's, that's true in most cases, I think; and that is what we are now experiencing in the South, is this initial response of bitterness, which I hope will be transformed into a, a more brotherly attitude. We hope that the end will be redemption and reconciliation, rather than division. But this, it seems to me, is a necessary phase of the transition from the old order of segregation and discrimination to the new order of freedom and justice. And this should not last forever; it's just something that's natural right now, and as soon as we pass out of the shock period into the more creative period of adjustment I think that bitterness and ill will will pass away.

HEFFNER: This sounds, in a sense, to be—if I may say this—in a sense, to be a denial of the judicial process, saying "we will work"; the judicial process doesn't allow for the violent activity, the aggressiveness; and it means, in a sense, stepping outside—not outside the law—but outside that slow, step-by-step process that has been going on in the courts. Do you think, for instance, that the courts would have been moved to action that would have taken the place of your boycott in Montgomery, had you not acted? Do you think there could be a substitute for that kind of action?

KING: I think not. I, I think it was necessary to do it. I think it was, the time was ripe. And I don't think there could have been a substitute at that particular time.

HEFFNER: Do think that the judicial structure—

WARING: Mr. Heffner, I want to say something on that. I, I think undoubtedly the action that Mr. King and his friends took in Montgomery was fine, necessary, and effective. Remember, the courts don't go out as an executive branch of the government should and do things for you. The court declares what your rights are. And the court says to you: You're an American citizen. Now, of course if you're scared and hide in the closet and don't exercise the rights of American citizens the courts can't turn around and say: You've got to do it. The courts have declared the rights. And I think the Supreme Court decision of May 17, 1954, was the greatest thing that's happened in this country in many, many decades. And I think that it declared, it declared, in effect, that segregation, legal segregation, segregation by law is illegal and not a part of the American system. And all the people, the big people and the little people throughout this land have awakened to the fact that they have a right. Now remember this: it's not a matter of giving rights. Rights aren't given. The right to vote isn't given to you. It's yours and it belongs to you. And the Negro people are beginning to realize that they are ordinary human beings and American citizens and they have these rights. And the courts have told them so. Now it's up to them to move out. They haven't got to go out with guns and bombs and gas, but they've got to go out with determination and courage and steadfastness like this man Luther King has done, and say: Here am I, and I stand here on my rights. And it's going to prevail; it's got to prevail; and it can't be beaten if we have enough of them who are steadfast enough. When they begin to compromise and sell out on principles, then they're gone. Now the matter of strategy is to keep a complete, solid front. There may be tactics as to whether you, you want to make bus cases first or school cases or railroad cases or things of that kind—those are minor details. But the strategy is: you must never surrender any of the rights you have gained, and you must look forward to the attainment of full equality.

HEFFNER: Well, I know that's your strategy. What about future tactics? Where do you go from here?

KING: Well, that's a pretty difficult question to answer at this point, since in Montgomery we have not worked out any future plans, that is, in any chronological order. We are certainly committed to work and press on until segregation is nonexistent in Montgomery and all over the South. We are committed to full equality and doing away with injustice wherever we find it. But as to the next move I don't have the answer for that because we have not worked that out at this point. We, I guess, have been so involved in the bus situation so that we have not had the real time to sit down and think about next moves. But in a general sense, we are committed to achieving first-class citizenship in every area of life in Montgomery and throughout the Southern community.

HEFFNER: But to what extent? This is a question that occurred to me, I wondered, to what extent the judicial decision of May, 1954 stimulated a greater feeling of self-respect amongst Negroes and intensified in them a willingness to assert their demands.

KING: I think it had a tremendous impact and influence on the Negro and bringing about this new self-respect. I think it certainly is one of the major factors, not the only—I think several other forces and historical circumstances must be brought into the picture. The fact that circumstances made it necessary for the Negro to travel more, so that his rural, plantation background was gradually supplanted by a more urban, industrial life—illiteracy was gradually passing away—and with the growth of the cultural life of the Negro, that brought about new self-respect. And economic growth, and also the tremendous impact of the world situation, with people all over the world seeking freedom from colonial powers and imperialism, these things all came together, and then with the decision of May 17, 1954, we gained the culminating point. That, it seems to me, was the final point which came to bring all of these things together. And that gave this new Negro a new self-respect, which we see all over the South and all over the nation today.

HEFFNER: Well, if this was a final point, in a sense, a culminating point, why do you ask now for another act on a national level, an act, let's say, on the part of the president, for a speech in the South? Why is this so important? Haven't enough steps been made up to this point to enable you to carry the ball from here on?

KING: Well, I think it's necessary for all of the forces possible to be working to implement and enforce the decisions that are handed down by the courts. And so often in the area of civil rights it seems that the judicial branch of the government is fighting the battle alone. And we feel that the executive and legislative branches of the government have the basic responsibility. And at points these branches have been all too silent and all too stagnant in their moves to implement and enforce the decisions. With the popularity of the president and his tremendous power and influence, just a word from him could do a great deal to ease the situation, calm emotions, and give southern white liberals something to stand on, if it is nothing but something to quote. The southern white liberal stands in a pretty difficult position because he does not have anywhere to turn for emotional security similar to what hate groups—I mean the things that other groups have to turn to—the hate organizations, so to speak. But with a word from the president of the United States, with his power and influence, it would give a little more courage and backbone to the white liberals in the South who are willing to be allies in the struggle of the Negro for first-class citizenship.

HEFFNER: To what extent—let me ask you this question, Judge Waring—are white Southerners willing to be allies in the battle of the new Negro?

WARING: That's a very hard question to answer. There are very, very few that are willing to come out in the open and say so. There are a great many, in my opinion, who would be glad if they were made to do it. I think that there are lots of people—I sometimes use the expression, that the little boy with the dirty face won't go and wash it, but if you grab him by the neck and scrub his face he then boasts that he has the cleanest face in the land. And I think there are many of the people in the South, and I saw many of them—my experience was that officially I was quite hated and condemned because I had expressed my views of what I thought the laws of the land were. And I got a lot of telephone messages and anonymous letters saying they agreed with me but they couldn't tell me why or how or who they were. And those people want to be free, but the overall picture of the politician—no politician in the South is going to dare come out and take this position of his own volition. But if the president of the United States tells him to, he's going to fall in line. And if we can get the top executive people to take action we'll get somewhere. Remember this, now: the Supreme Court has laid down the law and said what's constitutional. Now that's important, that's most important, it's the biggest thing that's ever happened. But it's got to be activated, it's got to be worked out, and the executive department has got to manipulate and work it and enforce it. And the legislative department should give the executive department more power to work and enforce these laws.

HEFFNER: You feel that action has to be taken on this level?

KING: Oh yes, very definitely.

HEFFNER: Let me ask again, though, about the feelings of the southern whites. How do you evaluate—if you had to give a progress report, how would you evaluate the battle you've fought over this past year? In terms of southern feelings, in terms of northern white feelings, too?

KING: Well, I think we've been able to see mixed emotions at this point. For instance, from a national point of view, looking all over the nation, we have had tremendous response and real genuine sympathy from many, many white persons, and naturally we've had the sympathy of Negroes. But many, many white persons of goodwill all over the nation have given moral support and a great deal of encouragement, and that has been very encouraging to us in the struggle. Now in the south—I guess the lines are more closely drawn—you find, on the one hand, a group more determined now than ever before because it is a last-ditch struggle, to do anything, even if it means using violence, to block all of the intentions and the desires of the Negroes to achieve first-class citizenship. But there are also others who have expressed sympathy. There are white Southerners, even in Montgomery, who have been quite sympathetic; as Judge Waring just said, sometimes these people, because of fear, refuse to say anything about it. They stand back because of fear of economic, social, and political reprisals. But there is a silent sympathy. And we have seen a great deal of that in Montgomery. So it's two sides. There's this side where you get the negative response, the other side where you have the positive response. And I have seen both. And I think as time goes on the negative side will get smaller and smaller. And those who are willing to be open-minded and accept the trend of the ages will grow into a majority group rather than a minority.

HEFFNER: You don't feel that there will be any violent reaction then over a long-range point of view to the progress that has been made?

KING: No, I don't. I think the violence will be temporary. Maybe . . . I don't say it will end tomorrow . . . we will go through some more for the next few months or so, but I think once we are over the shock period, that shock will be absorbed and Southerners will come to the point of seeing that the best thing to do is sit down and work out these problems and do it in a very Christian spirit. I think the violence that we are undergoing now is indicative of the fact that the diehards realize they are standing at the dying point. That is, the system is at its dying point. And that this is the last way to try to hold on to the old order.

WARING: Mr. Heffner, all these reforms have periods of trouble. Gandhi was murdered, Jesus was crucified, and you find that most great reforms have certain periods of stress and distress. Now, just one last point I want to make. When we speak of the laws, it is terribly important that they bring these cases and have a declaration of law, and action by Congress and action by the executive. Because now, up to the time of the Supreme Court's decision, segregation was legal. And segregation, even people of goodwill themselves, said that: the law says that we have to keep these people separate. For instance, it has been illegal for me to ride in a bus with Mr. King here. Now I don't want a law which says I've got to ride with him, or he's got to ride with me. But I don't want a law which says I can't sit in a seat with him. And we've broken that, and that's an enormous advance. And we've got to do it on every stage right down the line. The Congress of the United States, I believe—and I've been very cynical and skeptical about it—but I'm beginning to believe they're going to do a little something this time. And if they do a little something— they haven't done anything in seventy-five years—if they do a little something this time they'll do a little more next year, and the president of the United States and the officials in the administration will begin to see that if Congress is moving it's good politics to move, and that'll have a great motivating product on the national picture. I think we're going forward, we're going forward inexorably. We've got to win. And it's a question of whether we're going to win in a short time or a long time. I'm for the short period.

HEFFNER: How do you project this into the immediate future?

KING: Well, I . . . When I think of the question of progress in the area of race relations I prefer to be realistic, and when I say that I mean I try to look at it not from the pessimistic point of view or the optimistic, but rather from the realistic point of view. I think we've come a long, long way, but we have a long, long way to go. But it seems to me that if we will press on with determination, moral courage, and yet wise restraint and calm reasonableness, in a few years we will reach the goal. I have a great deal of faith in the future and the outcome. I am not despairing.

HEFFNER: And I'm sure as long as we have men like you, we can all have faith. Thank you so much.

WARING: So am I.

HEFFNER: Reverend King and Judge Waring.

"ADVICE FOR LIVING"

EBONY
MAY 1958

EBONY READER 1: I have a sixteen-year-old daughter by a previous marriage. My present husband doesn't like my daughter and my daughter doesn't like him. He is always picking on her. It has gotten to a point where either my husband or my daughter must go. It is impossible for the three of us to live together. Should I divorce my husband?

KING: I do not think a divorce is the answer to your problem. It would only create new and more complicated problems, especially with reference to your own personal adjustment. A better approach to the problem would be to seek to bring about a degree of understanding between your daughter and your husband. People fail to get along with each other because they fear each other. They fear each other because they don't know each other. They don't know each other because they have not properly communicated with each other. This is probably the case with your daughter and husband. They have probably never known each other nor properly communicated with each other. If you can bring them together and urge them to honestly discuss their differences and confess their mistakes, wherever they have been made, this, I believe, will go a long, long way toward restoring a broken relationship.

***EBONY* READER 2:** I am a white man (so-called), who is interested in the Negro's fight for equality. I am a NAACP member, but it seems to me that the organization is an exclusive club: people can join but there is no forum for expressing individual opinions. I live in New York. Where can white people go to help, what can individuals do in this fight for freedom?

KING: It is certainly commendable that you have such a passion for freedom and human dignity, that you are in quest for an organization through which you can best express your interest. You mentioned the NAACP as an organization which lacks the resources to serve as the proper channel through which your interest can flow. I would suggest that you reconsider your attitude toward the NAACP; it seems to me that the NAACP always leaves the way open for individuals to express opinions through the various branches. This organization has done more to achieve the legal and constitutional rights of Negro citizens than any other organization to which I can point. I feel that continued support of this organization is one of the ways that people of goodwill can further extend the rights of Negro Americans. Since you are in New York, you may very easily familiarize yourself with the resources, methods, and techniques of the NAACP by consulting the national office. Of course there are numerous other organizations working for the rights of Negroes, and many of them are doing exceptionally good jobs. There are organizations in the South, for instance, that are working on the local level to implement the decisions that the NAACP has won through the courts. These organizations are in dire need of financial and moral support. You may consider giving assistance to some of these organizations.

EBONY READER 3: My problem is my mother and my half brothers and sisters. My mother gives them all her attention. She takes them out, buys them pretty clothes. She never notices me. Her other children are light-skinned. I am dark. What can I do to make her love me, too?

KING: You can probably best deal with your problem by beginning with an analysis of self. I know this sounds rather strange to you, since you have already concluded that your mother and half-brothers and sisters are responsible for the problem. But you must honestly ask yourself the question, whether the problem has arisen because of an inferiority complex that you have developed as a result of your complexion. You must be sure that you do not unconsciously develop a bitterness because of your color, and thereby drive persons away from you. Maintain a wholesome attitude at all times and a radiant personality. These qualities, I am convinced, will awaken within those around you a responding attitude of kindness.

EBONY READER 4: I am a single woman, in my forties. I have a small business, but I am not pretty. My friends tell me they wish I could find a husband. So do I, but where is the man who is looking for anything else besides beauty? Don't good

morals and knowing how to make a home and an honest dollar count?

KING: Your desire to find a husband is certainly a normal and
reasonable one, and I hope our generation hasn't come to the
point that men only look for external beauty in a wife. A marriage that is only based on external beauty lacks the solid rock
of permanence and stability. One must discover the meaning
of soul beauty before he has really discovered the meaning of
love. I quite agree with you that good morals, and knowing how to make a home and an honest dollar are the things
that ultimately count in making a meaningful relationship.
Whether or not you will find the man who has the wisdom to
appreciate these values over against the passing value of physical beauty, I am not prepared to say. But at least you can live
by the assurance that you have cultivated in your life those
great imperishable values that are ends within themselves.

EBONY READER 5: I am a housewife and the mother of two
children. I have found out that many Negroes have inferiority
complexes, especially about their looks. It starts when they
are children. The stories they are told—Goldilocks, Black
Sambo—and the pictures they see play down the Negro. Are
there any children's stories, fables, or religious stories that
contain Negro characters?

KING: It is certainly true that many Negro children grow up
with inferiority complexes. This is basically true because they
grow up in a system which forever stares them in the faces saying, "You are less than," "You are not equal to." Segregation

generates a feeling of inferiority in the segregated. This sense of inferiority comes into being as a result of segregation. This sense of inferiority is further generated, as you suggest, by the inferior roles played by Negroes in pictures that they see and the stories that they read. It must be admitted that American society has done far too little in presenting the Negro in a realistic role. The stereotype role in which he has been traditionally presented is distasteful to any well-thinking Negro. Fortunately many things are happening to change this trend. More and more through television, movies, and other public channels, Negroes are being presented in a realistic manner and their creative abilities are increasingly coming to the forefront. This remains a real challenge for Negro artists and entertainers as well as writers.

DOES SEGREGATION EQUAL INTEGRATION?

INTERVIEW WITH MIKE WALLACE
PREVIOUSLY UNPUBLISHED
JUNE 25, 1958

The following transcript of an interview with Mike Wallace was found in Wallace's papers after his death and has never before been published in its entirety.

WALLACE: It has been said that most Negroes, the majority of Negroes are rather indifferent to the whole problem. What is your reaction to that?

KING: I am not sure if that is totally true. It is true that you don't have any universal response. You have so many different segments of Negro life that it is very difficult to get all Negroes to respond in a certain way. Many of them are indifferent for various reasons. It was different in Montgomery. There you had a smaller community, communication was easier in a community of 50,000 people. This is different from having to deal with 17 million in an entire nation. In Montgomery, we were in the midst of a crisis which brought us together. A crisis tends to do that. We had geographical limitations and numerical limitations but it was easier than it would have been on a national scale. I don't think Negroes generally are disinterested.

On the whole Negroes are quite concerned about it. It is just a matter of being involved in various things and maybe we have not, on a national scene, gotten down to the grass roots, down to the masses. This is the next move in Negro leadership.

WALLACE: Would you say that what happened in Montgomery is an ideal pattern for what will happen on a larger scale?

KING: Very definitely. I would like to see this a pattern all over. I think it is the only way we are going to speed up the coming of this new order through mass militant non-violent action on the part of the Negroes.

WALLACE: You said in Montgomery that what inspired this was a crisis, involving all the Negroes. But this involves all the Negroes in the country. You say that they are not indifferent, but it would appear that so many of them are indifferent. For example, where they are allowed to vote, the voting isn't anything to boast about.

KING: I don't deny that at all. That's a problem not only in the South. You have communities in the South where Negroes don't have any difficulty but it is just a problem of internal apathy. There again, the system has something to do with that. There is such a thing as freedom of exhaustion. That's a temptation you just—you just live under this thing so long that you adjust to it. There was a Negro in Atlanta, in a slum area, who used to play a guitar and sing this song called "Been Down So Long that Down Don't Bother Me." That's the freedom of exhaustion. He just broke down under the load. That has happened to many Negroes. The feeling that you have to fight all the time so that you adjust to conditions as they are. But you have another group of Negroes that want to gain freedom and all that goes along with it but they are not willing to bear the sacrifices involved. You have three groups actually. The first is completely indifferent, if you can call them indifferent. I would rather call them the people who have completely adjusted to conditions as they are. This is a small percentage. I would not think it is more than 10 or 15 percent. A second group of individuals are those who are determined—or at least concerned—about first-class citizenship and integration, but they are not willing to confront the sacrifices involved. Some of them are afraid because they are in vulnerable positions. Many Negro school teachers are in this second group. They are concerned but they would not attend a meeting of the NAACP. They believe in the NAACP, they want to see it come, but because of their positions, they just don't push it. That's a very large group. In that group also, you have a few people who really have a vested interest in segregation. Some Negroes profit by segregation.

WALLACE: Who?

KING: Some from an economic point of view. This is a small group also. Not a large group at all. There are those who feel that they cannot compete in an integrated society. So that some people who have made all their economic security on the basis of the system of segregation [have] the feeling that integration will break down these possibilities, a feeling that they cannot compete.

WALLACE: Do you mean a lawyer or a doctor?

KING: Not necessarily lawyers and doctors. I refer more to business people. Morticians, for example, will fit into this category. Even a few real estate people in the South.

WALLACE: Of the second large group, who would like to see himself furthered but will not take the trouble or risk? What percentage of Negroes?

KING: That's difficult to say. I would think this group is small, too. You don't have too many Negro professional people in any community.

WALLACE: No. I am talking about the large group.

KING: Well, I am referring to a lot of professional people—not more than 10 or 15 percent. I think you have at least between 60 or 70 percent of the Negroes of America who are determined to gain freedom and first-class citizenship. They are willing to make the sacrifices and they are just waiting for the guidance and leadership. They are ready. This includes the so-called masses. People who don't have education and economic security. But they are tired of the old order and they have revealed themselves. This is a majority group.

WALLACE: You said Montgomery is an ideal pattern of what should happen all over the country. How can this be done? You say 60 percent are waiting for it to be done.

KING: We must do it through leadership and organization. Bringing leaders together from all over the country. There is one organization now—the Southern Christian Leadership Conference, an organization that grew directly out of the Montgomery situation and through which we seek to bring together leaders from all of the major communities in the South to discuss the common problems and ways of implementing the Supreme Court decision through non-violent methods. We are now mainly concerned with voting. This is a time to get this pattern all over the South and get communities organized and get the Negro organized all over.

WALLACE: Right now there is going on a concerted attempt to get Negroes to pull bus strikes, boycotts, and the like?

KING: I wouldn't say that. I am sure that these things will come under discussion as the organization grows. It is still in its embryonic stages. We are now moving towards organization structure. We will just get into some of these problems in a more systematic fashion. The Southern Christian Leadership Conference consists of 190 leaders from 10 Southern states. They issued a statement and called to the president to meet with Negro leadership. It was this request that resulted in the meeting with the president the other day. This is an example of what the organization has done.

WALLACE: Are you personally satisfied with the progress made, particularly with Southern Negroes fighting for their rights? Many people have said this. Just what is to come pretty soon? The Negro specifically?

KING: I am sure we can do much more. No. I am not totally satisfied. This is the job ahead. To get this over the Negroes in all communities that the only way to do it is to organize, and as you know, I believe firmly in non-violence and in organizing. We must make the principle of non-violence our central principle. We must organize and prepare ourselves for militant and social action which is non-violent. So I am not totally satisfied with what we have done. We can do much more. If integration is to be a reality, the Negro will have to take the primary responsibility. All groups must work together, but the Negro himself must take primary responsibility.

WALLACE: Are you satisfied with the NAACP and with what they have done? Do you think there is room for major improvement? Are they on the wrong track?

KING: I don't mind that question because I think the NAACP is doing a good job in a manner of—the NAACP has achieved excellence in the area of legal strategy and is doing an excellent job in that area. Breaking down legal barriers to integration.

WALLACE: What about other areas?

KING: The NAACP recognizes that it cannot do the whole job. I have heard very responsible leaders from the Board of the NAACP say that the NAACP cannot do this job alone. What we seek to do through the Southern Christian Leadership Conference is to supplement the NAACP. Once you get your decisions from the Court, this isn't enough. You've got to implement it. What we can do in the South is take the noble decisions that have been rendered as a result of the work done by the NAACP and implement them on the local level through non-violent means.

WALLACE: You met with Eisenhower early this week. Last year you said that the executive level of government is apathetic on this problem. Do you think President Eisenhower personally or our administration is helping this cause very much?

KING: I wouldn't put it all on Eisenhower. I would say there is a great deal of apathy in both the legislative and executive branches of the government.

WALLACE: Why?

KING: I don't know. I am sure there are many reasons why. I don't know all of the reasons why there is apathy. Sometimes maybe it is due to the fact that persons in these positions do not understand the problem and the dimensions of it and what it is doing to our nation.

WALLACE: I am including the men in the legislative and executive branches who say they are all for civil rights, etc. Do you think many of them really care about Negroes?

KING: What persons are you speaking of?

WALLACE: The people in our government, the verbal champions of civil rights. Do you think they really care?

KING: I think some of them do. I think some of them have moral convictions about it. Some of them do it for political advantages. I am sure that some of them are serious and sincere. I don't doubt their motives at all. I think when Senator [Herbert H.] Lehman talks about it, he is sincere. He's a statesman. Senator [Paul] Douglas is sincere. He says a moral issue is involved. I think some others will do it for political advantage. They see it is politically expedient and they use it.

WALLACE: Can you conceive of Negroes and whites in America living together in harmony as one human being with another without there being a real feeling deep down inside that this is so. I know a lot of people who pay lip service but when it comes down to the real thing, like sending your kid to school where there are Negroes, or like your son bringing home his Negro friend, then it becomes a different story. As long as this feeling exists, are you going to achieve anything?

KING: I would hope that it can be achieved. So long as you have prejudiced attitudes and you have segregation in the country, you will have these attitudes all over the country. It touches the whole country. As we move through the transitions in the South, it is more intense in the South. I certainly feel that the problem can be solved if we meet it with moral strength. Injustice anywhere is a threat to justice everywhere. Justice everywhere sheds light on the problem of injustice in other areas. Now we are in this period where you do have people who have doubts even in northern communities. Even they have paid lip service to it. They are not committed to it absolutely.

WALLACE: Harry Ashmore says it is the law of the land and we should obey it. He never says this is a good thing and we whites should welcome the opportunity to sit in a classroom with other human beings.

KING: A deeper thing is this. You are saying in substance that many people will go along and will accept this because it is the law of the land but really they don't accept it because it is good? This is what I would call the distinction between desegregation and integration. Desegregation breaks down the legal barriers and brings men together physically. In Montgomery, Alabama, the buses are desegregated but not integrated. Integration is a personal and intergroup feeling. We are moving through the process of desegregation, which is a necessary step to integration. We cannot get to integration before going through the process of desegregation where you have to break down through legal means. I think most people think it is right to abide by certain laws—like traffic laws, etc. Men finally grow to the point of habit of following these laws. In America we are moving through the period of desegregation and the physical barriers are being broken down—the legal barriers, that is. Naturally you will have this problem of people going on with this automatically because it is the law, but once they are brought together—you see, they hate each other because they fear each other, they fear each other because they don't know each other.

WALLACE: How far does this integration go? This Ideal state? David Lawrence says the underlying fear of white Southerners is interracial marriage. Arthur Crock wrote a whole column on the same thing. Isn't this the end step? If one looks at another person as a human being rather than what is the color of his skin, you will have mass intermarriage.

KING: I don't think you will have mass intermarriage. That isn't what the Negro wants basically. The thoroughly integrated society means freedom. When any society says that I cannot marry a certain person, that society has cut off a segment of my freedom. It hasn't given me the possibility of alternatives. In the final analysis, intermarriage has no relevance to this issue. Races don't marry, people do. It is an agreement between two people and either party can say no. There will be intermarrying, I am sure. But in societies where you have a good deal of integration, you don't have a large percentage intermarrying.

WALLACE: You yourself say that there is a difference between desegregation and integration in which people voluntarily and willingly mingle and look upon each other as human beings and not as Negro and white. Doesn't this lead inevitably to this? H. J. Mueller said that there is no doubt that slowly and surely the races are blending together. There is no such thing as a pure Negro in America any more. They have one-third white blood.

KING: Who's responsible for that? Do you know? The person who makes the most noise about intermarriage is responsible. Many of the loudest segregationists in the South have fathered children by Negro women and the fear is a fear of retaliation. A sense of guilt.

WALLACE: Yes, that is the cause up to now. In the entertainment industry, amongst intellectual circles where this fear of Negro, white, Chinese is being diluted simply because people are integrated, you do find more and more interracial marriage.

KING: I am sure that integration will lead to some intermarriage. I don't deny that. I don't think this is the primary thing that the Negro is seeking. If you will go down any list of desires and wants of Negroes of American society, intermarriage was almost always at the bottom. Jobs, equal opportunity, education were at the top of the list.

WALLACE: This would reflect the conscious desires?

KING: Yes. Are you saying that this is a sub-conscious desire?

WALLACE: I am saying what people are saying. They point to statistics.

KING: My position is—I can state it in two points. First, properly speaking, individuals marry and not races. Second, that in communities where you have a great deal of integration, the percentage of interracial marriages will remain small.

WALLACE: Would you consider it bad if there were vastly increased interracial marriages provided that these were wholesome marriages? Would you consider it a bad thing for American society if these marriages increased?

KING: I don't know. I would have to think about that a little more. I wouldn't want to make a hasty statement on that. I have certain views still turning around in my mind on this whole issue. On that particular point, I have not come to a definite conclusion and I would rather not comment on that.

WALLACE: What effect do you think the recent court decision is going to have on both Negroes and whites in the South?

KING: It depends on the ultimate outcome. It is still in the process of litigation. It would depend on the outcome. If the decision isn't reversed, I think it can do two things. First, for the white South, it can become a sort of example and a pattern for them to follow. It is sort of a green light for foreign elements. It gives them a map to follow. Organized groups can go into areas and just cause a little trouble and this will be the pattern. If the decision is reversed, it would be helpful. It is crucial if we are to continue in the line of progress that the decision be reversed. Not just for Little Rock. This will become the pattern throughout the South. It seems to be both dangerous and tragic. The failure to reverse this decision might well depend on the justice of our nation. The civil rights issue will largely determine the effectiveness of America from now on in its international relationship.

WALLACE: Why?

KING: Because you have in this world about 1 billion 600 million colored peoples living in Asia and Africa. Most of them have lived under the yoke of colonialism for years and are now gaining their independence. American will never gain the respect of these growing new nations in the world so long as she has second-class citizenship.

WALLACE: What about the argument that desegregation is resulting in an intolerable atmosphere inside the schools?

KING: Well, one—if the forces of goodwill were as strong as they should be and conscientious and vocal, you wouldn't have as much tension in these situations. If in Little Rock the forces of goodwill were as strong as the forces of ill will, this would not have happened. I don't think the majority of the people felt that this should happen. The second thing is this. I cannot conceive of a period of social transition without some tension. This is inevitable. Whenever you are moving from an old order to a new order, in the transition period, there is some tension. We seek to lessen the tension as much as possible but we don't seek due process in order to avoid tension. We have a choice in America to move toward the goal of justice in spite of the tension it will create or stop the process in an attempt to avoid tension while in reality we are tearing away the very core of our nation. This is the choice. The one we should choose? Allow the inevitable tension to arise. There can be no birth or growth without birth and growing pains. Whenever you confront the new, there is the recalcitrance of the old, a response that shall develop. In any community where integration occurs, you are going to have this. We would not be integrated in Montgomery, Alabama if we had taken this attitude. We were determined to ride those buses on an integrated basis. Now it has worked out. Tension isn't the permanent condition of things. We have got to press on and realize that this tension is a necessary phase of the transition and when this transition is fulfilled, it will lead us to a greater democracy and a greater nation.

WALLACE: Was the Montgomery bus strike a very carefully planned supported strike? It has been said that you were a man set up as a figurehead but that this was really organized outside of Montgomery. What is your reaction?

KING: I don't know that a greater indigenous movement has ever taken place in America. There was nothing in terms of outsiders—first it was the NAACP, then it was the Communists. You hear this type of thing in the South. The only thing I can say is that it was a spontaneous movement developed by the Montgomery people who were tired of the indignities, etc. that they had suffered for many years on the buses. It was organized by the people of Montgomery, the leaders. It was a spontaneous response to an incident which was the arrest of Mrs. Rosie. This was merely the precipitating factor, not the causal factor. That lies deep down in the past, a long accumulation of humiliating experiences.

WALLACE: Will these small actions bubble up all over the South?

KING: I think so. I don't think Montgomery is the end of the process at all. Bus integration has taken place in many cities without the necessity of a bus strike. The pattern of Montgomery in this respect didn't have to repeat. New Orleans, Miami, Nashville all integrated their buses. Immediately after the decision came down in our case, several southern cities integrated without any statement. One or two of them said we don't want another Montgomery.

WALLACE: The example of Montgomery put the fear of God into white communities elsewhere?

KING: Yes. I think so. I think Montgomery can serve as a pattern not only in the bus integration but in other areas. It refutes the one thing that Negroes lived on for many years— that is that Negroes could not get together, organize, and unify on anything worthwhile.

WALLACE: Do you see any real integration in Montgomery as a result of desegregation?

KING: I don't think it is coming in the next year or two. Realism impels me to admit that it is going to take time. And a lot of hard work. A real possibility exists. It will depend on whether the Negro community will continue to move on or live in a negative past. That is possible in Montgomery or any community. You can talk about what happened in the past and get bogged down by the glory of your great yesterday and fail to see the challenges of tomorrow. If you continue to press on as you move on, you are moving toward integration in some form.

WALLACE: Does it depend upon the white people moving on?

KING: It depends upon both. I am convinced that the white people are not going to move on if the Negroes don't. It is going to depend on whether we continue to move, and our method in moving will arouse the consciences of the white people. Montgomery did a lot to awaken the decent consciences of the white people.

WALLACE: Do you think there are many consciences among the white people in the South?

KING: Oh yes. More than you can ever tell because you hear the noise of the extremists and they tend to drown out these persons of goodwill but they are there. But the hope is that something will happen through Negro voting so that people of goodwill can get into public positions.

WALLACE: In the white South, there are not only elements that want to desegregate but elements that want to be friends?

KING: You don't have a solid South regionally. You have three South's. The South of compliance—Oklahoma, Kansas, Missouri, West Virginia. The wait-and-see South—North Carolina, Tennessee, Texas, Florida, Arkansas. Then the recalcitrant, hard-core, resistant South—Alabama, Mississippi, Georgia. There are several South's in terms of attitudes. You have the white south that says we will do anything to maintain segregation, including physical violence. They are in the minority. You have another group that will say I don't believe that integration is morally sound but it is the law and we will follow it because of the law. This is the adjusted group in the south. Another group, small but growing, is made up of persons working toward integration. They believe this is morally and constitutionally sound. And there are many others—not just one.

WALLACE: Does the church play a part in this?

KING: We have a right to look to leadership in the church. This is basically a moral problem and the church is supposed to be the guardian of the morals of the community. The church is the just, organized institution in the South. Southerners are quite religious from an institutional point of view. They go to church on Sunday. I see some hope in that area. I think the churches are becoming much more conscious in this problem than ever before. The ministers that say integration is morally sound are so few. The majority group believe firmly in integration, and this is the gospel but if they are too vocal they feel that they will lose the churches. The church will immediately call the segregationists to the pastor. Response will be better in the long run. They can influence the mass of the young people in their day-to-day talks. Some people are willing to stand up and lose a church and be damned, if necessary. It is my idea on even liberalism, if we can use that word. I am afraid that we don't have enough people in America really committed to integration, not in terms of intellectual assent. Intellectual assent is merely agreeing that something is true. Not really living it. I am afraid that we don't have enough people in high places committed to it. I think President Eisenhower is a man of genuine integrity and goodwill, but on the question of integration he doesn't understand . . . how this problem is to be worked out, and the dimensions of social change. He thinks it will work itself out in years. I don't believe he thinks that segregation is the best condition of society. I think he believes it would be a fine thing to have an integrated society but I think he probably feels that the more you push it, the more tension it will create, so you just wait fifty or one hundred years and it will work itself out. I don't think he feels like being a crusader for integration.

WALLACE: In the 1960 election campaign, do you see any difference in 1960 as compared with 1956 regarding the integration or race problem?

KING: I would have to think about that a little more because I don't profess to have too much political ability and knowledge. I wouldn't go out endorsing either party. I see shortcomings in both and good points in both. As far as the Negro vote, I don't know. There can be a change, a swing to the Republican Party. But it will be determined by the action of the executive branch of the government to a large extent on this whole civil rights struggle. I mean President Eisenhower's behavior between now and 1960. But not only him. The Justice Department, too. I mean the whole executive branch. It is possible but it will not be a swing to the Republican Party just to make a change. There are other aims that the Negroes feel have been gotten through the Democratic Party.

FROM *WHO SPEAKS FOR THE NEGRO?*

**INTERVIEW WITH ROBERT PENN WARREN
MARCH 18, 1964**

WARREN: This is an interview, March eighteenth, with Dr. King. All right, sir. May I just plunge in and—

KING: —yes.

WARREN: —start with a topic and we'll explore it a little bit?

KING: All right.

WARREN: Do you see your father's role and your own role as historical phases of the same process?

KING: Yes, I do. I think my father and I have worked together a great deal in the last few years trying to grapple with the same problem, and he was working in the area of civil rights before I was born, and when I was just a kid, and I grew up in the kind of atmosphere that had a real civil rights concern. And I do think it's the—the same problem that we are grappling with. It's the same historical process, and if, if this is what you mean, I think so.

WARREN: That is, there are vast differences, of course, in techniques and opportunities and climate of opinion, all of those million things that are different from one generation to the other. But you see this, see a continuity in the process, and not a, not a sharp division between roles, yours and his?

KING: Yes, I see continuity. I, I don't think there's a sharp—there are certainly minor differences, but I don't think there is any sharp difference. I think basically the roles are the same. Now, I grant you that at points my father did not come up under the discipline of the non-violent philosophy. He was not really trained in the non-violent discipline, but even without that, the problem was about the same, and even though the methods may not have been consciously non-violent, they were certainly non-violent in the sense that he never advocated violence as a way to solve the problems.

WARREN: Yes, yes. Those are phases then, shall we say, in a process. What is the next phase one might envisage?

KING: You mean the next phase in terms of, of—

WARREN: —beyond, beyond the present leadership and the present issues and the present problems.

KING: Um-hm.

WARREN: Is there a phase beyond the civil rights issues that are now on the forefront? What is the next phase of, shall we say better—for the lack of a better phrase—the Negro movement?

KING: Um-hm.

WARREN: In a general sense?

KING: Yeah.

WARREN: What would be the next phase? Say, just, offhand saying your father representing one phase, you another. Can you predict a, another phase? Is that beginning to take shape already?

KING: Well, I think if there is a next phase it will be an extension of the present phase. My feeling is that we will really have to grapple with ways and means to really bring about an integrated society. Non-violent direct action, working through the courts, and working through legislative processes may be extremely helpful in bringing about a desegregated society. But when we move into the realm of actual integration, which deals with mutual acceptance, a genuine intergroup, interpersonal living, then it seems to me that other methods will have to be used. And I think that the next phase will be the phase that really grapples with the—the methods that must be used to bring about a thoroughly integrated society.

WARREN: In that phase, we can certainly see quite clearly responsibilities that belong to the white man, and obligations.

KING: Um-hm.

WARREN: Now, what problems, responsibilities, and

obligations would you say the Negro would have in this relationship in this third phase?

KING: Well, I would think this would be the phase, or the responsibilities of the Negro in this phase would be in the area [of] what Mahatma Gandhi used to refer to as "constructive work," his constructive program, which is a program whereby the individuals work desperately to improve their own conditions and their own standards. I think in this phase, after the Negro emerges in and from the desegregated society, then a great deal of time must be spent in improving standards which lag behind to a large extent because of segregation—

WARREN: —yes—

KING: —discrimination, and the legacy of slavery. But it seems to me that the Negro will have to engage in a sort of operation bootstraps in order to lift these standards. And I think by raising the, these lagging standards, it will make it much more, well, I, I would say much less difficult for him to move on into the integrated society.

WARREN: Have you followed the controversy between Irving Howe and Ralph Ellison in *Dissent* [and *The New Leader*]?

KING: No, I, I haven't.

WARREN: To fall into? It deals with this question of, say, a man like Ralph, who is outside the, of the picket lines—

KING: —um-hm—

WARREN: —being called up short by a white liberal saying, "You don't belong, as an art writer: you [??] to be carrying on a protest." Ralph's reply was in, in short, "You, Irving Howe, are another kind of Bilbo. You want to put me in my place that you have picked out for me and not let me be the kind of writer I want to be."

KING: Um-hm. Um-hm.

WARREN: That's already [??] I'm [asking] an aspect of the third phase, which is now.

KING: Yes, I think so. I think that one has to recognize that this—[*telephone ringing*]—could you hold?

[*Pause in recording.*]

KING: I've forgotten where I was.

WARREN: Well, I put out a question, but I think we'd—

KING: —uh-hm—

WARREN: —come to a point of pause there. Two weeks ago a prominent newspaperman said to me—a Southerner by birth—"Thank God for Dr. King; he's our only hope." He was worrying about violence. Now, this is very often said by white people. Dr. Kenneth Clark has remarked, in print, that your appeal to many white people is because you lull them into some sense of security. And I hear, too, that there is some resistance, automatic emotional resistance, on the part of Negroes because they feel that your leadership has somehow given a, not quote "sellout," but a sense of a soft line, a rapprochement that flatters the white man's sense of security. Do you encounter this, and how do you, how do you think about this? How do you feel about these things, assuming they are true?

KING: Well, I don't agree with it. [*Laughs*] Naturally. I think, first, one must understand what I'm talking about and what I'm trying to do when I say "love," and that the love ethic must be at the center of this struggle. I'm certainly not talking about an affectionate emotion. I'm not talking about what the Greek language would refer to as "Eros," or—

WARREN: —yes—

KING: —*famil*. I'm talking about something much deeper. And I think there's a misunderstanding.

WARREN: But, now, how can this misunderstanding be cleared up? I know your writings and I've heard you speak on, on that. But a misunderstanding somehow remains among a large segment of Negroes and among a large segment of whites.

KING: Um-hm. Um-hm. Well, I don't think it can be cleared up for those who refuse to look at the meaning of it. I've done it.

WARREN: I see.

KING: I've said it in print over and over again.

WARREN: Yes, you have. Yeah.

KING: But I do not think violence and hatred can solve this problem.

WARREN: Yes.

KING: I think they will end up creating many more social problems than they solve, and I'm thinking of a very strong love. I'm not, I'm thinking, I'm thinking of love in action and not something where you say, "Love your enemies," and just leave it at that, but you love your enemies to the point that you're willing to sit-in at a lunch counter in order to help them find themselves. You're willing to go to jail.

WARREN: Yes.

KING: And I don't think anybody could consider this coward-ice or even a weak approach. So I think—

WARREN: —yes—

KING: —that many of these arguments come from, from those who have gotten so caught up in bitterness that they cannot see the deep moral issues involved. That you're—

WARREN: —or the white man, caught up in complacency.

KING: Yes.

WARREN: Refuses to understand it.

KING: Yes, I think so. I think both.

WARREN: Let me shove ahead since we're so pressed and I have—

KING: —um-hm. [*Laughs*]

WARREN: Don't laugh. Speaking of bitterness and the pining for bitterness, let's take the Reconstruction of the South after the Civil War as a, a tragic shoring up of all kinds of, of bitternesses and unresolved problems. Myrdal, in his big work, gives what he considers a sketch for what would have been a reasonable Reconstruction as you, no doubt, recall. The first item he puts on his list would've been compensation to slaveholders by the federal government for the emancipated slaves. Second, expropriation of land held by Southern planters with payment. Then the selling of land to both Negroes and whites who were landless—

KING: —um-hm.

WARREN: Selling on a long-time basis and other factors. How do you emotionally respond to this question of paying the Southern slaveholder for the slaves emancipated by the Civil

War, during the Civil War? Do you find an emotional resistance to that? How do you, how do you respond to that?

KING: Well, I don't find too much emotional resistance to it. I do feel that the Reconstruction period was an unf—a tragic period at points because many of the social problems we face today are here because this period was not used properly. It wasn't planned properly, and the future wasn't looked at properly in dealing with the present situations then. I don't, I don't know if this would have been a way of solving the problem, but I don't have any emotional resistance to the idea if, if there was as much concern about seeing that the landless slaves and the penniless slaves had some kind of compensation and something to start with, maybe this plan would've worked all right because it would have given both a sense of dignity, and maybe the bitterness that we now face—still face—at many points wouldn't be there because the start would've been a little better.

WARREN: That undoubtedly is what Myrdal was, was driving at, this hypothetical situation.

KING: Yeah.

WARREN: But I had discovered this, this question, giving Myrdal, who's an objective foreign commentator.

KING: Um-hm.

WARREN: This passage sometimes evokes very violent

responses from Negroes who are thoroughly acquainted with history, you know.

KING: Um-hm.

WARREN: People of cultivation and—

KING: —yeah—

WARREN: —and, and decent feelings, on the first two counts there, will have violent emotional responses.

KING: Um-hm. Yeah. Well, mine is the same way. I'm not, I'm not saying that I agree that this was the way to solve the problem, but I do feel that after 244 years of slavery, certain patterns had developed in the nation, and certain attitudes had developed in the minds of people all over the nation that everybody had to take some of the responsibility for this sin committed. And consequently, in solving the problem, it seems to me, maybe some things would have had to be done which may not have represented everything that we would want to see, but it may have saved us many of the bitter moments that we have now.

WARREN: You wouldn't have felt, then, that this somehow would've been a betrayal of your dignity as a Negro human being to have had this compensation paid? This is all hypothetical of course. But you would not emotionally respond in that way?

KING: Well, I, I would think that the whole system, my, my revolt and my emotional response is so much over the, the tragedy of the whole system of slavery that I would revolt against that as much as over the fact that slavery existed for all of these years, you see.

WARREN: Sure, sure. That's, that, that question is a, is a, is the question behind it all?

KING: Yes. Yeah. But I don't, I don't absolutely feel that this was a way to solve the problem, but yet I, I don't have this strong emotional feeling of bitterness when I hear it suggested because we had accumulated a social problem which had to be grappled with, and this was merely a suggestion as one of the ways that it may have been dealt with, and, and may have saved us some of the problems now. Whether it would have, we don't know!

WARREN: We don't know. It's hypothetical.

KING: Yeah. That's right.

WARREN: But would it have been possible to implement it—

KING: Unless—

WARREN: —given a war psychology in '65 in the North is another question, too.

KING: —is another, that's right. Exactly.

WARREN: Let me try something else, another general question. All revolutions, as far as I know, in the past, have had the tendency, even the expressionist tendency, to move toward a centralized leadership—

KING: —um-hm—

WARREN: —to move toward a man who has both a power and symbolic function.

KING: Um-hm.

WARREN: Now you are stuck yourself in a very peculiar role by a series of things, personal qualities and God knows what else, you know. But still there is no—[*pause*] this revolution, if we call it one, does, is not following that pattern, though we see the tendency to focus on single leadership. Can a revolution survive without this symbolic focus, even if not without, even without a literal focus under single leadership?

KING: I think so.

WARREN: You, you know the question. I mean I'm might not, I'm not putting it well, but you get what I'm driving at?

KING: Yes, I think, I think I do. I think a revolution can survive without this single centralized leadership, but I do think there must be centralized leadership in the sense that, say, in our struggle, all of the leaders coordinate their efforts, cooperate, and, and at least evince a degree of unity. And I think if we, say, if all of the major leaders in this struggle were at, at war with each other, then I think it would be very difficult to make this social revolution the kind of powerful revolution that it's proved to be. But the fact is that we have had, on the whole, a unified leadership, although it hasn't been just one person. And I think there can be a collective leadership. Maybe some symbolize the struggle a little more than others, but I think it's absolutely necessary for the leadership to be united in order to make the revolution effective.

WARREN: There's a problem that many people now talk about, from now on as more and more activity occurs in the big centers like Harlem and Detroit and Chicago, desperate wondering as to whether any leadership now visible or imaginable can control the random explosion that might come at any time—

KING: —um-hm—

WARREN: —the random violence—

KING: Yeah. Well—

WARREN: —that is stored; it's being stored up because we know it's stored up.

KING: Um-hm. Yes.

WARREN: Is that the big central problem you all are facing now?

KING: Well, I think it's a, it's a real problem. And I think the only answer to this problem is the degree to which the nation is able to go; I should say the speed in which we move toward the solution of the problem. The more progress we can have in race relations and the, the more we move toward the goal of an integrated society, the more we lift the hope, so to speak, of the masses of people. And it seems to me that this will lessen the possibility of sporadic violence. On the other hand, if we get setbacks and if something happens where the Civil Rights Bill is watered down, for instance, if the Negro feels that he can do nothing but move from one ghetto to another and one slum to another, the despair and the disappointment will be so great that it will be very difficult to keep the struggle disciplined and non-violent. So I think it will depend on the rate of progress and the speed, and recognition on the part of the white leadership of, of the need to go on and get this problem solved and solved in a hurry, and the need for massive action programs to do it.

WARREN: Let me read a quotation from Mr. Galamison about the schools and the boycott.

KING: Um-hm. Um-hm.

WARREN: "I would rather see it"—the public school system— "destroyed than not conform to," and then another quote, "to his timetable of integration." And "Maybe it has run its course, anyway"—the public school system.

KING: Maybe it's? I didn't get the last part.

WARREN: "Maybe the public school system has run its course anyway."

KING: Oh, uh-hm.

WARREN: It's over.

KING: Um-hm.

WARREN: He'd rather see it destroyed than not conform to his prescribed timetable—

KING: —um-hm—

WARREN: —for integration.

KING: And you, you're asking what about?

WARREN: How, how do you respond to, to that statement?

KING: Well, I don't think the public school system has run its course, far from it. And I don't think that we should think in terms of the destruction of the system. I—I tend to feel that we can rectify the system by constantly bringing this issue to the forefront of the conscience of the nation or of our communities. I think the school boycott idea is a very good one. I think it's one of the creative ways to dramatize an intolerable condition. But I wouldn't go to the point of saying that I would like to see the school system destroyed. I think what he is probably getting at is that as long as you have inferior and segregated school systems, you, you aren't getting a quality education for anybody whether it's Negro or white. I agree with the Supreme Court at this point that separate facilities are inherently unequal, and somehow the segregated gets a false sense of inferiority because of these very separate facilities. So the—

WARREN: —that's—I'm sorry, please.

KING: No, I was just going to say, so that I would, I would say that the real need is to fight hard to get the system rectified and not to destroy the public schools.

WARREN: Let's take a case like this. [And I don't say this] With any polemical intent, you see. It's just a question of the kind of problem.

KING: Sure. Yeah.

WARREN: Let's take Washington, D.C., or New York City if things go as they're now going, with a concentration of Negro population in the cities—

KING: —um-hm—

WARREN: —and almost a vast majority of public school students then being Negroes.

KING: Um-hm.

WARREN: How can you integrate, say, Washington, D.C., if you have 95 percent or 90 percent of the schools, your public schools, are Negro? Where do you get the white kids to integrate them with?

KING: Well, you—

WARREN: —what could be done there?

KING: —you have two problems here. One is the fact that this problem will never be ultimately solved until the housing problem is solved. As long as there is residential segregation and as long as the whites in the central city run to the suburbs and leave these core areas, you do have a real problem. Now the only way that it can be dealt with in the transition while we are trying to solve the problem of housing discrimination through various means is to, to transfer students from one district to another, the busing system.

WARREN: Suppose they don't have it. Suppose Washington, D.C., as a total unit, has only, say, 85 percentage of its Negro students in the, up to the eighth grade or the twelfth grade or whatever it would be. Where do you get the white students to bus in? Can you go to Virginia or West Virginia to get them?

KING: Well, in a case like that you do have a real problem. I think it, it's a, I guess the Washington situation is almost unique because many of these people live in Virginia and Maryland and even in other states, and that makes the problem even more difficult.

WARREN: What about New York where, the way it's moving—the problem is becoming that way in New York.

KING: Yeah, but there, on the whole, people are still in New York City. I mean they're, sometimes they're in, say, Westchester County. They may be in, in the Queens, some area of the Queens, but, but still I, I could see it working a little better—

WARREN: —a little better—

KING: —in a situation like that.

WARREN: But the problem is we're dealing with a prin—, as a principle, where you can, can see situations where it's insoluble transfer.

KING: Yeah. Well, I agree with you.

WARREN: Then what do we do?

KING: I agree that, that the problem will not be ultimately solved. There are these insoluble situations where we have to, we, we, we have to, we have to see that problem solved in, in the run of history when we get housing integration on a broad level. And I think that this is an area where we must work as hard, you know, to solve the problem of residential segregation as we do to integrate the schools. However, where, wherever schools can be integrated through the busing method, and where it won't be just a, a terrible inconvenience, I think it ought to be done because I think the inconveniences of a segregated education are much greater than the inconveniences of busing students so that they can get an integrated, quality education.

WARREN: Are you referring to white and Negro students both, in this matter of—

KING: —that's right—

WARREN: —of inconvenience? Both are being short-changed, as it were?

KING: That's right. Oh, yes. Yes, exactly.

WARREN: It's not just the Negro being given a chance to be with a white child or going to a better school, it's the question of the white child's own relationship to himself and to Negroes, too?

KING: That's right. In other words, my, I feel that when a white child goes to school only with white children, unconsciously that child grows up in many instances devoid of a world perspective. There is an unconscious provincialism, and it can develop into an unconscious superiority complex just as a Negro develops an unconscious inferiority complex. And it seems to me that one must, that our society must come to see that this whole question of, of integration is not merely a matter of quantity, having the same this and that in terms of a building, or a desk, or this, but it's a matter of quality. It's, if I can't communicate with a man, I'm not equal to him. It's not only a matter of mathematics; it's a matter of psychology and philosophy.

WARREN: Well, he isn't equal to you either if he can't communicate with you.

KING: Exactly. It's the same, the same thing.

WARREN: It cuts both ways.

KING: It cuts both ways, exactly.

WARREN: Let me ask a question that lies behind part of this, I think, at least for some people it lies behind it.

KING: Um-hm.

WARREN: Dubois, many years ago spoke about this, wrote about this, the split or the possible split in the Negro psyche. The Negro pulled, on one hand, toward almost a mystique of African heritage, or at least the special Negro cultural heritage here, to the mystique of blackness, to all of this. On the other hand the pull toward Western European Judaic-Christian American cultural heritage, with the penalty there, or the price or what, of being absorbed away from the other cultural heritage, even having the blood integrity lost entirely, possibly, in the end?

KING: Um-hm. Um-hm.

WARREN: The sense of some betrayal somehow hidden in here? Does this problem present itself to you as a real problem, as a real issue, or not?

KING: Well, it's a real issue, and I think it, it has made for a good deal of frustration in the Negro community, and people have tried to solve it through various methods. One has been to try to reject, psychologically, the, anything that reminds you of your heritage, you know, and, and this is particularly true of the Negro middle-class, the desire to reject anything that reminds you of Africa, anything that, really anything that reminds you of the masses of Negroes, and then trying to identify with the white majority, the white middle-class. And so often what happens is that this individual finds himself caught out in the middle with no cultural roots because he's rejected by so many of the white middle-class, and he's out here right in the middle with no cultural roots and he ends up, as E. Franklin Frazier says in a book, "unconsciously hating himself" when he tries to compensate for this through conspicuous consumption. So it, there's no doubt about the fact that this has been a problem, but I don't think it has to be. I think one can live in American society with a certain cultural heritage, whether it's an African heritage or other, European, what, what have you, and still absorb a great deal of this culture. There is always cultural assimilation. This is not an unusual thing; it's a very natural thing. And I think that we've got to come to see this. The Negro is an American. We, we, we know nothing about Africa, although our roots are there in terms of our forbearers. But I mean, as far as the average Negro today, he knows nothing about Africa. And I think he's got to face the fact that he is an American, his culture is basically American, and one becomes adjusted to this when he realizes what, what he is. He's got to know what he is. Our destiny is tied up with the destiny of America.

WARREN: Some anthropologists and sociologists say that the American Negro is more like the old American, the old New Englander or the old Southerner, like any other kind of American.

KING: Um-hm.

WARREN: Does this make sense to you?

KING: I think so. I think, I think they're probably quite correct there.

WARREN: Did you read Faulkner's *Intruder in the Dust*, that novel fifteen years ago?

KING: No, I didn't. I know of the novel—

WARREN: —yes, of course—

KING: —very well but I didn't read it.

WARREN: He has a passage there where he talks of somehow—and in a very cryptic way—of a homogeneity in the

South involving both the Southern white man and the Southern Negro as having some homogeneity against, some rapport against an outside order of society.

KING: I'm not sure I understand what he means. Do you?

WARREN: Well, nobody's quite sure what it means.

KING: Um-hm.

WARREN: But that somehow, let's pose the question another way. A young lady at Howard, who's a very brilliant girl and stands high in law school and has been on a lot of picket lines and jails, too, she's, can do other things, said to me a few months ago, she had great hope for a settlement in the South because of a common history between the, the white man and the Negro. And she said being on the land over this period of time has given some human recognition, even at [??].

KING: Um-hm.

WARREN: That the possibility of a rapprochement, an understanding in the end. She said, "I'm frightened by Harlem or Detroit. I don't see the possibility of the human communication." She was raised on a farm in Virginia, she said. She didn't say [??] involved here. Now, she is not in a sense soft, you see. She's been in jails, you see? Does this make any sense?

KING: Well, I think that this may be some truth here. I feel, for instance, that in the South you have a sort of contact between Negroes and whites, an individual contact, that you don't have in the North, for instance. Now, this now is mainly a paternalistic thing, you know. It's a law of servantry—

WARREN: —or a billyclub.

KING: Yes.

[*Tape 1 ends; tape 2 begins.*]

WARREN: This is tape two of the interview with Dr. King. Continue.

[*Pause in recording.*]

WARREN: Let me ask you this. Can we go—

[*Pause in recording.*]

WARREN: We can, all right. Good. That's great. What about the meaning of "Freedom Now," the slogan "Freedom Now"? We know the historical process is never now, and it's never absolute.

KING: Um-hm.

WARREN: What about the relation between the historical process and the slogan?

KING: Yes. Well, I think the slogan is a good one, and I think it—it really means that the Negro has reached the point of feeling that he should have freedom now. Now, I don't think there's any illusion in the mind of anybody about the fact that you've got to observe historical process, you've got to think about the fact that this structural change cannot come overnight. But we must work at it and we must try to deal with it with such an urgency that we do have, we are challenged by the, the need for it now. And, and I think this is more of a challenge to work and realize the urgency of the moment than it is a belief that you can really get freedom within, within such a short period.

WARREN: I sat with a group of students some months ago and asked if it's a question of social process.

KING: Um-hm.

WARREN: And a very bright boy, a senior in a good college, said, "I understand about social process, in time," he said, "but I can't bear to bring myself to say it."

KING: Um-hm.

WARREN: Closed his eyes and—

KING: —yeah, well, I find it is a problem. And we have lived so long with this idea, with people saying it takes time and wait on time, that I find it very difficult to, to adjust to this. I mean, I, I get annoyed almost when I hear it, although I know it takes time. But the people that use this argument have been people so often who, who really didn't want the change to come, and gradualism for them meant a do-nothing-ism, you know, and the standstill-ism, so that it has been a revolt, I think, against the idea of a feeling, on the part of some, that you can just sit around and wait on time when actually time is neutral. It can be used either constructively or destructively.

WARREN: But some words have become symbolically charged with feelings where they can't even be used, where they mean the same thing as other words.

KING: Yes. Yes, exactly.

WARREN: Like the word "gradual" has become emotionally charged, symbolically charged—

KING: —that's right.

WARREN: So the word can't be used.

KING: That's right. Exactly.

WARREN: When you say "historical process," it's—it's, the word's been cleaned though it means the same thing.

KING: It means the same, identical thing, but all of the emotions, you know, surrounding gradual, gradualism, that, and—and this whole thing of waiting on time, it—it brings about an initial resentment from, from the Negro and his allies in the white community.

WARREN: Now, speaking of symbolisms like that, symbolic charging and other ends of things, I was talking a few weeks ago with a very, very able Negro attorney, and he suddenly said, "I live in a society"—he's a very violent, bitter man.

KING: Um-hm.

WARREN: But very able—I live in a society where all the symbolism of the poetry I read, the, the Bible I read, is charged with the white man's values. "God's white robes," you know, a—

KING: —um-hm—

WARREN: "—white light of hope, you know, all of the, which I, which are an affront to me." And he said, "I find myself schooling myself now to resist all the symbolism and invert it for myself."

KING: Um-hm. Um-hm. Yeah. Well, I think this is, many Negroes go through this, and, and I think now probably more than ever before. My only hope is that this kind of reaction will not take us right back where we, you know, into the same thing we're trying to get out. There's always a danger that an oppressed group will seek to rise from the position of disadvantage to one of advantage, you see, thereby subverting justice, so that you end up substituting one tyranny for another. Now, I think our danger is that we can get so bitter that we revolt against everything white, and this becomes a very dangerous thing because it, it can lead to the kind of philosophy that you get in the black Nationalist movements, and the kind of philosophy that ends up preaching black supremacy as a mean, as a way of counteracting white supremacy. And I just think this is a, this would be bad for our total society. But I can well understand the kind of, of, the kind of impatience and the psychological conditions that lead to this kind of reaction.

WARREN: It's there.

KING: Yeah.

WARREN: There's a special thing about this revolution that makes it unlike, as far as I can tell, any other. All previous revolutions have aimed at the liquidation of a class or a regime.

KING: Yes. Yes.

WARREN: This one does not aim at liquidation of a class or a regime.

KING: Um-hm. That's right. It's—

WARREN: —it's aimed at something else.

KING: It's a revolution.

WARREN: How, how would you define that aim then?

KING: Well, I would say that this is a revolution to get in. It's very interesting. I think you're quite right that most revolutions, almost all revolutions, have been centered on destroying something, you see, and that's been the center. When in this revolution, the whole quest is for the Negro to get into the mainstream of American life. He's, it's a revolution calling upon the nation to live up to what is already there in an id—, in an idealistic sense, I mean in all of its creeds and all of its basic affirmations, but it's never lived up to it. So I think this is the difference. It is a revolution of rising expectations, and it is a revolution not to liquidate the structure of America, but a revolution to get into the mainstream of American life.

WARREN: A revolution to liquidate an idea, is that it?

KING: That's right, to liquidate an idea which is out of harmony with the basic idea of the nation.

WARREN: It's a new kind of revolution.

KING: It's, yes, it's, it's a revolution, it is a new kind of revolution.

WARREN: Now, let me say it and you can say it correctly or, revise—

KING: —yeah. I, I'll get it. I got it. Yeah.

WARREN: Correct or revise this. The problem may be, is this your problem and, and people like yourself, to define this revolution in the new terms to contain the element of hate and liquidation and exploit the element of hope? All of it is based on hope and hate together. They're the dynamics—

KING: —um-hm—

WARREN: —in the revel of—

KING: —um-hm—

WARREN: —change, revolutionary change.

KING: Um-hm. Um-hm.

WARREN: You want to drive one horse, not two, unless you want to kill one of the horses.

KING: Yes. Yes. And you are saying, now, you, you're saying that—

WARREN: —hate's a great dynamic in a revolution.

KING: Yes. Yes, but what you're saying is that in this revolution, you don't, you don't have this?

WARREN: You have it psychologically, sure.

KING: Yes.

WARREN: That's human.

KING: I, yeah.

WARREN: The hate element is there.

KING: Um-hm.

WARREN: But it's a question of containing that.

KING: Yeah.

WARREN: Or converting it to something else—

KING: —yes—

WARREN: —because there's no legitimate object for it.

KING: Um-hm. Um-hm.

WARREN: It can't [aim at] Liquidation.

KING: Yes. Yes. Well, I think you're quite right, and I think that this is a part of the job of the leadership in this revolution, you know, to keep that hope alive, and yet keep this, this kind of, I guess, the word "hate" here. The best way I would call it is to keep the kind of righteous indignation alive, or the kind of healthy discontent alive, that will keep the revolution moving on because we don't—

WARREN: —without the personal focus?

KING: Without the personal. Yes, I think that's right.

WARREN: Is that it?

KING: That's right.

WARREN: Let me ask you one, one more question. How do you interpret the assaults on you in Harlem?

KING: That, you mean—

WARREN: —the two assaults, yeah—

KING: —the two, the—

WARREN: —yes, yes.

KING: The stabbing and the—

WARREN: —two, stabbing and the, the throwing of things. These two experiences must have been ghastly shocking, of course, to anybody—

KING: —um-hm.

WARREN: But as a special extra shock in—

KING: —yes—

WARREN: —your case.

KING: Yes. Yeah. Well, the first one, I, I don't know if we'll ever know what the cause or basis was because here you had a demented mind who really didn't know why she was doing it. I, I really don't, really don't think, it may be that she had been around some of the meetings of these groups in Harlem, black Nationalist groups, that have me all the time as a favorite object of scorn—

WARREN: —yes—

KING: —and hearing this over and over again, she, she may have responded to it when I came to Harlem. Or it may be that she was just so confused that she would've done this to anybody whose name was in the news. We, we'll never know. But now on the other one where they threw eggs at—

WARREN: —yes—

KING: —eggs at a car, I think that was really a, a result of the black Nationalist groups, and a feeling, you know, they've heard all of these things about my being soft and my talking about "love the white man" all the time, and I, I think a real feeling that, that, that this kind of approach is far from it, it's a cowardly approach. And they transfer that bitterness toward the white man to me because they began to see, I mean, they began to fear that I'm saying love this person that they have such a bitter attitude toward. I think it's, I think it grows right out of that. In fact, Malcolm X had a meeting the day before and he had talked about me a great deal and said, told them that I would be there the next

night and said, "Now, you all are to go over there and let
old King know what you think about him." And he had said
a great deal about non-violence, criticizing non-violence,
and saying that I approved of Negro men and women being
bitten by dogs and the fire hoses, and I say, say go on and
not defend yourself. So I think this kind of response grew
out of the build up and the, all of the talk about my being a
sort of polished Uncle Tom. I mean this is the kind of thing
they say in those groups. Now, my feeling has always been,
again, that they have never understood what I've said, I'm,
I'm saying—

WARREN: —same old story?

KING: Because, yeah, they confuse, they don't see that there's
a great deal of a difference between nonresistance to evil and
non-violent resistance. And certainly I'm not saying that you
sit down and patiently accept injustice. I'm talking about a
very strong force, where you stand up with all your might
against an evil system, and you, you, you are not a coward.
You, you, you are resisting, but you've come to see that tacti-
cally, as well as morally, it is better to be non-violent. I can't
see anything, but even if one would, didn't want to deal with
the moral questions, it would just be impractical for the Negro to talk about making his struggle a violent one.

WARREN: On that point, the, this Brinkley survey and the
Post survey in Harlem came up with an astonishing fact, that
a large percentage of the population of Harlem do not think
of a Negro as being a minority.

KING: Is that so?

WARREN: Don't even know it.

KING: They don't even—

WARREN: —that even though it's factually been done.

KING: Yeah.

WARREN: And other, others feel it, emotionally don't feel it because they see so few white people around.

KING: This is a, that's right; they never go out of Harlem.

WARREN: So, the tactical appeal doesn't apply to them.

KING: Um-hm. Yeah.

WARREN: They say, "We're the majority."

KING: Yeah. That's right. That's right. I think that's—

WARREN: —that's dangerous fact, isn't it?

KING: Right. That's a dangerous fact, yes. And, you see, many people in Harlem never go out of Harlem. I mean, they'd never even been downtown. And you can see how this bitterness can accumulate. Here, you see people crowded and hovered up in ghettos and slums with no hope, you see. They,

they, they see no way out. If they could, you know, look down a long corridor and see an exit sign, they would feel a little better, but they, they see no sense of hope. And it, it's, it's very easy for one talking about violence and hatred for the white man to appeal to them. And, and I have never thought of this, but I think this, this is quite true, that if, even if you talk to them about non-violence from a tactical point of view, they can't quite see it because they don't even know they're outnumbered—

WARREN: —that's right—

KING: —you see.

WARREN: Emotionally, they can't grasp it.

KING: That's right. They can't grab it.

WARREN: Let me ask one more question. When you were assaulted, and it's very hard, I know, to reconstruct one's own feelings, what did you feel? What were your first actual reactions at the moment they threw the, well, say the eggs and so forth, say that, that, not the mad woman, but the, the other. Can you reconstruct that?

KING: Well, I—

WARREN: —was it significant to you in a, in an emotional way what you went through in that moment?

KING: Yes, I remember my feelings very well. I, at, at first this was a very, I guess I had a, a very depressing response because I realized that these were my own people, these were Negroes throwing eggs at me. And I guess you do go through those moments when you begin to think about what you're going through and the sacrifices and suffering that you face as a result of the movement, and yet your own people don't have an understanding and are seeking, not even an appreciation, and seeking to destroy your image at every point. But then it was very interesting. I went right into church and I spoke and I started thinking not so much about myself but about the very people, the society that made people respond like this. It was so interesting how I was able very quickly to get my mind off of myself and feeling sorry for myself and feeling rejected, and I started including them into the orbit of my thinking that it's not enough to condemn them for doing this, this, engaging in this act, but what about the society and what about the conditions that are still alive which made people act like this? And I got up and spoke and mentioned this, and the people were almost, they didn't, I told them about the ex-perience because many of them in the church didn't know about it and I got up and told them, and they were, they didn't quite know how to respond when I said, I told them what happened and I said, "But, you know, the thing that concerns me is not so much the, those young men. I feel sorry for them. I'm concerned about the fact that maybe all of us have contributed to this by not working harder to get rid of the conditions, the poverty, the social isolation, and all of the conditions that cause individuals to respond like this.

WARREN: I've attended some of your meetings; I was at Bridgeport two weeks ago.

KING: Oh, you were?

WARREN: Yes. And I was struck by one fact. It was a total middle-class audience, wasn't it? Middle-class?

KING: Yeah, I think it was, by and large.

WARREN: Middle-class audience.

KING: Yes. Yes.

WARREN: By and large that.

KING: Um-hm.

WARREN: Now you have, I've never seen, except in that context I never see you in a situation where you're dealing with a mass audience, you see—

KING: —um-hm—

WARREN: —of, of the uneducated and the poorly educated and the poor.

KING: Um-hm. Um-hm.

WARREN: I should like to see that sometime at one—

KING: —oh, yes—

WARREN: —of these gatherings.

KING: Yes. Well, I—

WARREN: —I know you have—

KING: —I do it a great deal—

WARREN: —these types of experiences. I know you do.

KING: Yes. Yes.

WARREN: But if you ever have—

KING: Even when I'm going, sometimes when we're in a city having a direct action program, I will go into poolrooms and many of the taverns, and just have a session there where I speak to groups.

WARREN: I know that's true. Friends of mine have been with you to see you do it.

KING: Um-hm.

WARREN: So I know it happens.

KING: Yes.

WARREN: I'd just like to see that sometime—

[*Tape 2 ends.*]

[*End of interview.*]

CONVERSATION WITH MARTIN LUTHER KING

68TH ANNUAL CONVENTION OF THE
RABBINICAL ASSEMBLY
MARCH 25, 1968

This is a transcript of Martin Luther King, Jr.'s responses to questions, which had been submitted in advance to his interlocutor, Rabbi Everett Gendler.

Professor Abraham Joshua Heschel introduced Dr. King to the assembled rabbis.

HESCHEL: Where does moral religious leadership in America come from today? The politicians are astute, the establishment is proud, and the marketplace is busy. Placid, happy, merry, the people pursue their work, enjoy their leisure, and life is fair. People buy, sell, celebrate, and rejoice. They fail to realize that in the midst of our affluent cities there are districts of despair, areas of distress.

Where does God dwell in America today? Is He at home with those who are complacent, indifferent to other people's agony, devoid of mercy? Is He not rather with the poor and the contrite in the slums?

Dark is the world for me, for all its cities and stars. If not for the few signs of God's radiance who could stand such agony, such darkness?

Where in America today do we hear a voice like the voice of the prophets of Israel? Martin Luther King is a sign that God has not forsaken the United States of America. God has sent him to us. His presence is the hope of America. His mission is sacred, his leadership of supreme importance to every one of us.

The situation of the poor in America is our plight, our sickness. To be deaf to their cry is to condemn ourselves.

Martin Luther King is a voice, a vision, and a way. I call upon every Jew to harken to his voice, to share his vision, to follow in his way. The whole future of America will depend upon the impact and influence of Dr. King.

May everyone present give of his strength to this great spiritual leader, Martin Luther King.

KING: I need not pause to say how very delighted I am to be here this evening and to have the opportunity of sharing with you in this significant meeting, but I do want to express my deep personal appreciation to each of you for extending the invitation. It is always a very rich and rewarding experience when I can take a brief break from the day-to-day demands of our struggle for freedom and human dignity and discuss the issues involved in that struggle with concerned friends of goodwill all over our nation. And so I deem this a real and a great opportunity.

Another thing that I would like to mention is that I have heard "We Shall Overcome" probably more than I have heard any other song over the last few years. It is something of the theme song of our struggle, but tonight was the first time that I ever heard "We Shall Overcome" in Hebrew, so that, too, was a beautiful experience for me, to hear that great song in Hebrew.

It is also a wonderful experience to be here on the occasion of the sixtieth birthday of a man that I consider one of the truly great men of our day and age, Rabbi Heschel. He is indeed a truly great prophet.

I've looked over the last few years, being involved in the struggle for racial justice, and all too often I have seen religious leaders stand amid the social injustices that pervade our society, mouthing pious irrelevancies and sanctimonious trivialities. All too often the religious community has been a taillight instead of a headlight.

But here and there we find those who refuse to remain silent behind the safe security of stained glass windows, and they are forever seeking to make the great ethical insights of our Judeo-Christian heritage relevant in this day and in this age. I feel that Rabbi Heschel is one of the persons who is relevant at all times, always standing with prophetic insights to guide us through these difficult days.

He has been with us in many of our struggles. I remember marching from Selma to Montgomery, how he stood at my side and with us as we faced that crisis situation. I remember very well when we were in Chicago for the Conference on Religion and Race. Eloquently and profoundly he spoke on the issues of race and religion, and to a great extent his speech inspired clergymen of all the religious faiths of our country; many went out and decided to do something that they had not done before. So I am happy to be with him, and I want to say happy birthday, and I hope I can be here to celebrate your one-hundredth birthday.

I am not going to make a speech. We must get right to your questions. I simply want to say that we do confront a crisis in our nation, a crisis born of many problems. We see on every hand the restlessness of the comfortable and the discontent of the affluent, and somehow it seems that this mammoth ship of state is not moving toward new and more secure shores but toward old, destructive rocks.

It seems to me that all people of goodwill must now take a stand for that which is just, that which is righteous. Indeed, in the words of the prophet Amos, "Let justice roll down like the waters and righteousness like a mighty stream."

Our priorities are mixed up, our national purposes are confused, our policies are confused, and there must somehow be a reordering of priorities, policies, and purposes. I hope, as we discuss these issues tonight, that together we will be able to find some guidelines and some sense of direction.

GENDLER: We begin now with some of the batches of questions. And since the question of confusion came up, and the problem of politics, perhaps we can begin with two or three questions which are rather immediate and relate to some very recent developments. One question is, "At this point, who is your candidate for president?" One question is, "If as it now seems Johnson and Nixon are nominated, do you have any suggestions as an alternative for those seeking a voice in the profound moral issues of the day?" And a third question in this general area of immediacy, "Would you please comment on Congressman Powell's charge that you are a moderate, that you cater to Whitey, and also his criticism that you do not accept violence?" Some criticism!

KING: Well, let me start with the first question. That is relatively easy for me because I have followed the policy of not endorsing candidates.

Somebody is saying stand, so I guess I'll have to . . .

GENDLER: Might I say that since Dr. King anticipates a good bit of footwork next month, we thought perhaps this particular evening he could remain off his feet.

KING: I'll stand.

On the first question, I was about to say that I don't endorse candidates. That has been a policy in the Southern Christian Leadership Conference. We are a non-partisan organization. However, I do think the issues in this election are so crucial that it will be impossible for us to absolutely follow the past policy. I do think the voters of our nation need an alternative in the 1968 election, but I think we are in bad shape finding that alternative with simply Johnson on the one hand and Nixon on the other hand. I don't see the alternative there. Consequently, I must look elsewhere. I think in the candidacy of both Senator Kennedy and Senator McCarthy we see an alternative. It is not definite, as you know, that President Johnson will be renominated. Of course, we haven't had a situation since 1884 when an incumbent president was not renominated, if he wanted the nomination. But these are different days and it may well be that something will happen to make it possible for an alternative to develop within the Democratic Party itself.

I think very highly of both Senator McCarthy and Senator Kennedy. I think they are both very competent men. I think they are relevant on the issues that are close to our hearts, and I think they are both dedicated men. So I would settle with either man being nominated by the Democratic Party.

On the question of Congressman Powell and his recent accusation, I must say that I would not want to engage in a public or private debate with Mr. Powell on his views concerning Martin Luther King. Frankly, I hope I am so involved in trying to do a job that has to be done that I will not come to the point of dignifying some of the statements that the Congressman has made.

I would like to say, however, on the question of being a moderate, that I always have to understand what one means. I think moderation on the one hand can be a vice; I think on the other hand it can be a virtue. If by moderation we mean moving on through this tense period of transition with wise restraint, calm reasonableness, yet militant action, then moderation is a great virtue which all leaders should seek to achieve. But if moderation means slowing up in the move for justice and capitulating to the whims and caprices of the guardians of the deadening status quo, then moderation is a tragic vice which all men of goodwill must condemn.

I don't see anything in the work that we are trying to do in the Southern Christian Leadership Conference which is suggestive of slowing up, which is suggestive of not taking a strong stand and a strong resistance to the evils of racial injustice. We have always stood up against injustices. We have done it militantly. Now, so often the word "militant" is misunderstood because most people think of militancy in military terms. But to be militant merely means to be demanding and to be persistent, and in this sense I think the non-violent movement has demonstrated great militancy. It is possible to be militantly non-violent.

On the question of appealing to "Whitey," I don't quite know what the Congressman means. But here again I think this is our problem which must be worked out by all people of goodwill, black and white. I feel that at every point we must make it very clear that this isn't just a Negro problem, that white Americans have a responsibility, indeed a great responsibility, to work passionately and unrelentingly for the solution of the problem of racism, and if that means constantly reminding white society of its obligation, that must be done. If I have been accused of that, then I will have to continue to be accused.

Finally, I have not advocated violence. The Congressman is quite right. I haven't advocated violence, because I do not see it as the answer to the problem. I do not see it as the answer from a moral point of view and I do not see it as the answer from a practical point of view. I am still convinced that violence as the problematic strategy in our struggle to achieve justice and freedom in the United States would be absolutely impractical and it would lead to a dead-end street. We would end up creating many more social problems than we solve, and unborn generations would be the recipients of a long and desolate night of bitterness. Therefore, I think non-violence, militantly conceived and executed, well-organized, is the most potent weapon available to the black man in his struggle for freedom and human dignity.

GENDLER: Having raised several points that some of the questions referred to, we may proceed by a further exploration of some of these elements, Dr. King, and perhaps we could begin with several questions that relate to your evaluation of the internal mood of the black community.

Let me share some of the formulations of these questions with you: How representative is the extremist element of the Negro community? How do we know who really represents the Negro community? If we are on a committee and there is a Negro militant and a Negro moderate, how shall a concerned white conduct himself?

What is your view of the thinking in some Negro circles which prefers segregation and separatism, improving the Negro's lot within this condition? How do you see Black Power in this respect?

Black militants want complete separation. You speak of integration. How do you reconcile the two?

How can you work with those Negroes who are in complete opposition to your view, and I believe correct view, of integration?

KING: Let me start off with the question, "How representative are the extremist elements in the black community?" I assume when we say extremist elements we mean those who advocate violence, who advocate separatism as a goal. The fact is that these persons represent a very small segment of the Negro community at the present time. I don't know how the situation will be next year or the year after next, but at the present time the vast majority of Negroes in the United States feel that non-violence is the most effective method to deal with the problems that we face.

Polls have recently revealed this, as recently as two or

three months ago. *Fortune* magazine conducted a pretty in-
tensive poll, others have conducted such polls, and they reveal
that about 92 percent of the Negroes of America feel that there
must be some non-violent solution to the problem of racial injustice. The *Fortune* poll also revealed that the vast majority of
the Negroes still feel that the ultimate solution to the problem
will come through a meaningfully integrated society.

Now let me move into the question of integration and
separation by dealing with the question of Black Power. I've
said so often that I regret that the slogan Black Power came
into being, because it has been so confusing. It gives the wrong
connotation. It often connotes the quest for black domination rather than black equality. And it is just like telling a
joke. If you tell a joke and nobody laughs at the joke and you
have to spend the rest of the time trying to explain to people
why they should laugh, it isn't a good joke. And that is what
I have always said about the slogan Black Power. You have to
spend too much time explaining what you are talking about.
But it is a slogan that we have to deal with now.

I debated with Stokely Carmichael all the way down the
highways of Mississippi, and I said, "Well, let's not use this
slogan. Let's get the power. A lot of ethnic groups have power,
and I didn't hear them marching around talking about Irish
Power or Jewish Power; they just went out and got the power;
let's go out and get the power." But somehow we managed to
get just the slogan.

I think everybody ought to understand that there are
positives in the concept of Black Power and the slogan, and
there are negatives. Let me briefly outline the positives. First,
Black Power in the positive sense is a psychological call to

manhood. This is desperately needed in the black community, because for all too many years black people have been ashamed of themselves. All too many black people have been ashamed of their heritage, and all too many have had a deep sense of inferiority, and something needed to take place to cause the black man not to be ashamed of himself, not to be ashamed of his color, not to be ashamed of his heritage.

It is understandable how this shame came into being. The nation made the black man's color a stigma. Even linguistics and semantics conspire to give this impression. If you look in *Roget's Thesaurus* you will find about 120 synonyms for black, and right down the line you will find words like smut, something dirty, worthless, and useless, and then you look further and you find about 130 synonyms for white and they all represent something high, noble, pure, chaste—right down the line. In our language structure, a white lie is a little better than a black lie. Somebody goes wrong in the family and we don't call him a white sheep, we call him a black sheep. We don't say whitemail, but blackmail. We don't speak of white-balling somebody, but black-balling somebody.

The word "black" itself in our society connotes something that is degrading. It was absolutely necessary to come to a moment with a sense of dignity. It is very positive and very necessary. So if we see Black Power as a psychological call to manhood and black dignity, I think that's a positive attitude that I want my children to have. I don't want them to be ashamed of the fact that they are black and not white.

Secondly, Black Power is pooling black political resources in order to achieve our legitimate goals. I think that this is very positive, and it is absolutely necessary for the black people of America to achieve political power by pooling political resources. In Cleveland this summer we did engage in a Black Power move. There's no doubt about that. I think most people of goodwill feel it was a positive move. The same is true of Gary, Indiana. The fact is that Mr. Hatcher could not have been elected in Gary if black people had not voted in a bloc and then joined with a coalition of liberal whites. In Cleveland, black people voted in a bloc for Carl Stokes, joining with a few liberal whites. This was a pooling of resources in order to achieve political power.

Thirdly, Black Power in its positive sense is a pooling of black economic resources in order to achieve legitimate power. And I think there is much that can be done in this area. We can pool our resources, we can cooperate, in order to bring to bear on those who treat us unjustly. We have a program known as Operation Breadbasket in SCLC [Southern Christian Leadership Conference], and it is certainly one of the best programs we have. It is a very effective program and it's a simple program. It is just a program which demands a certain number of jobs from the private sector—that is, from businesses and industry. It demands a non-discriminatory policy in housing. If they don't yield, we don't argue with them, we don't curse them, we don't burn the store down. We simply go back to our people and we say that this particular company is not responding morally to the question of jobs, to the question of being just and humane toward the black people of the community, and we say that as a result of this we must withdraw our economic support.

That's Black Power in a real sense. We have achieved

some very significant gains and victories as a result of this program, because the black man collectively now has enough buying power to make the difference between profit and loss in any major industry or concern of our country. Withdrawing economic support from those who will not be just and fair in their dealings is a very potent weapon.

Political power and economic power are needed, and I think these are the positives of Black Power.

I would see the negatives in two terms. First, in terms of black separatism. As I said, most Negroes do not believe in black separatism as the ultimate goal, but there are some who do and they talk in terms of totally separating themselves from white America. They talk in terms of separate states, and they really mean separatism as a goal. In this sense I must say that I see it as a negative because it is very unrealistic.

The fact is that we are tied together in an inescapable network of mutuality. Whether we like it or not and whether the racist understands it or not, our music, our cultural patterns, our poets, our material prosperity, and even our food are an amalgam of black and white, and there can be no separate black path to power and fulfillment that does not ultimately intersect white routes. There can be no separate white path to power and fulfillment, short of social disaster, that does not recognize the necessity of sharing that power with black aspirations for freedom and justice.

This leads me to say another thing, and that is that it isn't enough to talk about integration without coming to see that integration is more than something to be dealt with in esthetic or romantic terms. I think in the past all too often we did it that way. We talked of integration in romantic and esthetic terms and it ended up as merely adding color to a still predominantly white power structure.

What is necessary now is to see integration in political terms where there is sharing of power. When we see integration in political terms, then we recognize that there are times when we must see segregation as a temporary way station to a truly integrated society. There are many Negroes who feel this; they do not see segregation as the ultimate goal. They do not see separation as the ultimate goal. They see it as a temporary way station to put them into a bargaining position to get to that ultimate goal, which is a truly integrated society where there is shared power.

I must honestly say that there are points at which I share this view. There are points at which I see the necessity for temporary segregation in order to get to the integrated society. I can point to some cases. I've seen this in the South, in schools being integrated, and I've seen it with Teachers' Associations being integrated. Often when they merge, the Negro is integrated without power. The two or three positions of power which he did have in the separate situation passed away altogether, so that he lost his bargaining position, he lost his power, and he lost his posture where he could be relatively militant and really grapple with the problems. We don't want to be integrated *out* of power; we want to be integrated *into* power.

And this is why I think it is absolutely necessary to see integration in political terms, to see that there are some situations where separation may serve as a temporary way station to the ultimate goal which we seek, which I think is the only answer in the final analysis to the problem of a truly integrated society.

I think this is the mood which we find in the black community, generally, and this means that we must work on two levels. In every city we have a dual society. This dualism runs in the economic market. In every city, we have two economies. In every city, we have two housing markets. In every city, we have two school systems. This duality has brought about a great deal of injustice, and I don't need to go into all that because we are all familiar with it.

In every city, to deal with this unjust dualism, we must constantly work toward the goal of a truly integrated society while at the same time we enrich the ghetto. We must seek to enrich the ghetto immediately in the sense of improving the housing conditions, improving the schools in the ghetto, improving the economic conditions. At the same time, we must be working to open the housing market so there will be one housing market only. We must work on two levels. We should gradually move to disperse the ghetto, and immediately move to improve conditions within the ghetto, which in the final analysis will make it possible to disperse it at a greater rate a few years from now.

GENDLER: Considering both the enlightenment and encouragement which I think many of us received just now from Dr. King's portrayal of the prevalent mood in the black community, we might move on to another complex of questions relating, Dr. King, to the prevailing mood in the black community which also would benefit from some clarification by you. This is what we might call the area of black and Jewish communal relations.

What steps have been undertaken and what success has been noted in convincing anti-Semitic and anti-Israel Negroes, such as Rap Brown, Stokely Carmichael, and [Floyd] McKissick, to desist from their anti-Israel activity?

What effective measures will the collective Negro community take against the vicious anti-Semitism, against the militance and the rabble-rousing of the Browns, Carmichaels, and [Adam Clayton] Powells?

Have your contributions from Jews fallen off considerably? Do you feel the Jewish community is copping out on the civil rights struggle?

What would you say if you were talking to a Negro intellectual, an editor of a national magazine, and were told, as I have been, that he supported the Arabs against Israel because color is all-important in this world? In the editor's opinion, the Arabs are colored Asians and the Israelis are white Europeans. Would you point out that more than half of the Israelis are Asian Jews with the same pigmentation as Arabs, or would you suggest that an American Negro should not form judgments on the basis of color? What seems to you an appropriate or an effective response?

KING: Thank you. I'm glad that question came up because I think it is one that must be answered honestly and forthrightly.

First let me say that there is absolutely no anti-Semitism in the black community in the historic sense of anti-Semitism. Anti-Semitism historically has been based on two false, sick, evil assumptions. One was unfortunately perpetuated even by many Christians, all too many as a matter of fact, and that is the notion that the religion of Judaism is anathema. That was the first basis for anti-Semitism in the historic sense.

Second, a notion was perpetuated by a sick man like

Hitler and others that the Jew is innately inferior. Now in these two senses, there is virtually no anti-Semitism in the black community. There is no philosophical anti-Semitism or anti-Semitism in the sense of the historic evils of anti-Semitism that have been with us all too long.

I think we also have to say that the anti-Semitism which we find in the black community is almost completely an urban Northern ghetto phenomenon, virtually non-existent in the South. I think this comes into being because the Negro in the ghetto confronts the Jew in two dissimilar roles. On the one hand, he confronts the Jew in the role of being his most consistent and trusted ally in the struggle for justice in the civil rights movement. Probably more than any other ethnic group, the Jewish community has been sympathetic and has stood as an ally to the Negro in his struggle for justice.

On the other hand, the Negro confronts the Jew in the ghetto as his landlord in many instances. He confronts the Jew as the owner of the store around the corner where he pays more for what he gets. In Atlanta, for instance, I live in the heart of the ghetto, and it is an actual fact that my wife in doing her shopping has to pay more for food than whites have to pay out in Buckhead and Lennox. We've tested it. We have to pay five cents and sometimes ten cents a pound more for almost anything that we get than they have to pay out in Buckhead and Lennox Square where the rich people of Atlanta live.

The fact is that the Jewish storekeeper or landlord is not operating on the basis of Jewish ethics; he is operating simply as a marginal businessman. Consequently the conflicts come into being.

I remember when we were working in Chicago two years

ago, we had numerous rent strikes on the West Side. And
it was unfortunately true that the persons whom we had to
conduct these strikes against were in most instances Jewish
landlords. Now sociologically that came into being because
there was a time when the West Side of Chicago was almost
a Jewish community. It was a Jewish ghetto, so to speak, and
when the Jewish community started moving out into other
areas, they still owned the property there, and all of the problems of the landlord came into being.

We were living in a slum apartment owned by a Jew in
Chicago along with a number of others, and we had to have
a rent strike. We were paying $94 for four run-down, shabby
rooms, and we would go out on our open housing marches
in Gage Park and other places and we discovered that whites
with five sanitary, nice, new rooms, apartments with five
rooms out in those areas, were paying only $78 a month. We
were paying 20 percent tax.

It so often happens that the Negro ends up paying a color
tax, and this has happened in instances where Negroes have
actually confronted Jews as the landlord or the storekeeper, or
what-have-you. And I submit again that the tensions of the
irrational statements that have been made are a result of these
confrontations.

I think the only answer to this is for all people to condemn injustice wherever it exists. We found injustices in the
black community. We find that some black people, when they
get into business, if you don't set them straight, can be rascals.
And we condemn them. I think when we find examples of
exploitation, it must be admitted. That must be done in the
Jewish community too.

I think our responsibility in the black community is to make it very clear that we must never confuse *some* with *all*, and certainly in SCLC we have consistently condemned anti-Semitism. We have made it clear that we cannot be the victims of the notion that you deal with one evil in society by substituting another evil. We cannot substitute one tyranny for another, and for the black man to be struggling for justice and then turn around and be anti-Semitic is not only a very irrational course but it is a very immoral course, and wherever we have seen anti-Semitism we have condemned it with all of our might.

We have done it through our literature. We have done it through statements that I have personally signed, and I think that's about all that we can do as an organization to vigorously condemn anti-Semitism wherever it exists.

On the Middle East crisis, we have had various responses. The response of some of the so-called young militants again does not represent the position of the vast majority of Negroes. There are some who are color-consumed and they see a kind of mystique in being colored, and anything non-colored is condemned. We do not follow that course in the Southern Christian Leadership Conference, and certainly most of the organizations in the civil rights movement do not follow that course.

I think it is necessary to say that what is basic and what is needed in the Middle East is peace. Peace for Israel is one thing. Peace for the Arab side of that world is another thing. Peace for Israel means security, and we must stand with all of our might to protect its right to exist, its territorial integrity. I see Israel, and never mind saying it, as one of the great outposts of democracy in the world, and a marvelous example of what can be done, how desert land almost can be transformed into an oasis of brotherhood and democracy. Peace for Israel means security and that security must be a reality.

On the other hand, we must see what peace for the Arabs means in a real sense of security on another level. Peace for the Arabs means the kind of economic security that they so desperately need. These nations, as you know, are part of that third world of hunger, of disease, of illiteracy. I think that as long as these conditions exist there will be tensions, there will be the endless quest to find scapegoats. So there is a need for a Marshall Plan for the Middle East, where we lift those who are at the bottom of the economic ladder and bring them into the mainstream of economic security.

This is how we have tried to answer the question and deal with the problem in the Southern Christian Leadership Conference, and I think that represents the thinking of all of those in the Negro community, by and large, who have been thinking about this issue in the Middle East.

GENDLER: Thank you very much, Dr. King. Perhaps we could share now a few questions relating to some of the domestic issues of poverty. A couple of them ask about the Kerner Report: If the Kerner Report recommendations are implemented, will it make a difference? What is your opinion of the report of the Kerner Commission?

Another raises the question of people of good intentions wanting to deal with slum problems and hardly knowing what to do, feeling that most of the simple tutoring and palliative efforts in the community may not amount to much, given the entire context of the system. It speaks of the power structure, the establishment finding funds for supersonic transports, moon projects, technological developments which are mere luxuries, for Vietnam, but not for those pressing needs which affect millions here at home. "Can you suggest why the establishment seems to work this way? Is it an accident or does it have deeper causes? What seem to you the minimal changes needed in the system in order to achieve some greater measure of social justice and equality?"

And perhaps related to this is the question of some of the realistic goals of the poor peoples' campaign to be held in Washington beginning April 22.

KING: Thank you. I want to start this answer by reiterating something that I said earlier, and that is that we do face a great crisis in our nation. Even though the president said today that we have never had it so good, we must honestly say that for many people in our country they've never had it so bad. Poverty is a glaring, notorious reality for some forty million Americans. I guess it wouldn't be so bad for them if it were shared misery, but it is poverty amid plenty. It is poverty in the midst of an affluent society, and I think this is what makes for great frustration and great despair in the black community and the poor community of our nation generally.

In the past in the civil rights movement we have been dealing with segregation and all of its humiliation, we've been dealing with the political problem of the denial of the right to vote. I think it is absolutely necessary now to deal massively and militantly with the economic problem. If this isn't dealt with, we will continue to move as the Kerner Commission said, toward two societies, one white and one black, separate and unequal. So the grave problem facing us is the problem of economic deprivation, with the syndrome of bad housing and poor education and improper health facilities all surrounding this basic problem.

This is why in the SCLC we came up with the idea of going to Washington, the seat of government, to dramatize the gulf between promise and fulfillment, to call attention to the gap between the dream and the realities, to make the invisible visible. All too often in the rush of everyday life there is a tendency to forget the poor, to overlook the poor, to allow the poor to become invisible, and this is why we are calling our campaign a poor peoples' campaign. We are going to Washington to engage in non-violent direct action in order to call attention to this great problem of poverty and to demand that the government do something, more than a token, something in a large manner to grapple with the economic problem.

We know, from my experiences in the past, that the nation does not move on questions involving genuine equality for the black man unless something is done to bring pressure to bear on Congress, and to appeal to the conscience and the self-interest of the nation.

I remember very well that we had written documents by the Civil Rights Commission at least three years before we went to Birmingham, recommending very strongly all of the things that we dramatized in our direct action in Birmingham. But the fact is that the government did not move, Congress did not move, until we developed a powerful, vibrant movement in Birmingham, Alabama.

Two years before we went into Selma, the Civil Rights Commission recommended that something be done in a very strong manner to eradicate the discrimination Negroes faced in the voting area in the South. And yet nothing was done about it until we went to Selma, mounted a movement, and really engaged in action geared toward moving the nation away from the course that it was following.

I submit this evening that we have had numerous documents, numerous studies, numerous recommendations made on the economic question, and yet nothing has been done. The things that we are going to be demanding in Washington have been recommended by the president's Commission on Technology, Automation and Economic Progress. These same things were recommended at our White House Conference on Civil Rights. The Urban Coalition came into being after the Detroit riot, and recommended these things.

The Kerner Commission came out just a few days ago recommending some of the same things that we will be demanding. I think it is basically a very sound, realistic report on the conditions, with some very sound recommendations, and yet nothing has been done. Indeed, the president himself has not made any move toward implementing any of the recommendations of that Commission. I am convinced that nothing will be done until enough people of goodwill get together to respond to the kind of movement that we will have in Washington, and bring these issues out in the open enough so that the Congressmen, who are in no mood at the present time to do anything about this problem, will be forced to do something about it.

I have seen them change in the past. I remember when we first went up and talked about a civil rights bill in 1963, right after it had been recommended by President Kennedy on the heels of the Birmingham movement. Mr. Dirksen was saying that it was unconstitutional, particularly Title I dealing with integrated public accommodations. He was showing us that it was unconstitutional. Yet we got enough people moving—we got rabbis moving, we got priests moving, we got Protestant clergymen moving, and they were going around Washington and they were staying on top of it, they were lobbying, they were saying to Mr. Dirksen and others that this must be done.

Finally, the Congress changed altogether. One day when Senator Russell saw that the civil rights bill would be passed and that the Southern wing could not defeat it, he said, "We could have blocked this thing if these preachers hadn't stayed around Washington so much."

Now the time has come for preachers and everybody else to get to Washington and get this very recalcitrant Congress to see that it must do something and that it must do it soon, because I submit that if something isn't done, similar to what is recommended by the Kerner Commission, we are going to have organized social disruption, our cities are going to continue to go up in flames, more and more black people will get frustrated, and the extreme voices calling for violence will get a greater hearing in the black community.

So far they have not influenced many, but I contend that if something isn't done very soon to deal with this basic economic problem to provide jobs and income for all America, then the extremist voices will be heard more and those who are preaching non-violence will often have their words falling on deaf ears. This is why we feel that this is such an important campaign.

We need a movement now to transmute the rage of the

ghetto into a positive constructive force. And here again we feel that this movement is so necessary because the anger is there, the despair is growing everyday, the bitterness is very deep, and the leader has the responsibility of trying to find an answer. I have been searching for that answer a long time, over the last eighteen months.

I can't see the answer in riots. On the other hand, I can't see the answer in tender supplications for justice. I see the answer in an alternative to both of these, and that is militant non-violence that is massive enough, that is attention-getting enough to dramatize the problems, that will be as attention-getting as a riot, that will not destroy life or property in the process. And this is what we hope to do in Washington through our movement.

We feel that there must be some structural changes now, there must be a radical re-ordering of priorities, there must be a de-escalation and a final stopping of the war in Vietnam and an escalation of the war against poverty and racism here at home. And I feel that this is only going to be done when enough people get together and express their determination through that togetherness and make it clear that we are not going to allow any military-industrial complex to control this country.

One of the great tragedies of the war in Vietnam is that it has strengthened the military-industrial complex, and it must be made clear now that there are some programs that we can cut back on—the space program and certainly the war in Vietnam—and get on with this program of a war on poverty. Right now we don't even have a skirmish against poverty, and we really need an all-out, mobilized war that will make it possible for all of God's children to have the basic necessities of life.

GENDLER: Because Dr. King must still meet tonight at least briefly with certain men from particular areas in the country, and be cause Reverend Young must also meet with some men from the Washington area immediately after this session, regretfully we have time for only one more question.

Although Dr. King is probably a bit weary and it is even conceivable that some of you are, I must say I very much regret that we haven't more time to pick up some of the supplementary questions. Yet we have time really for only one last question, and I should imagine that, knowing the mood of the Rabbinical Assembly, the final questions have been asked in these kinds of terms, Dr. King.

One is: What can we best do as rabbis to further the rights and equal status of our colored brethren? Another is: What specific role do you think we as rabbis can play in this current civil rights struggle? What role do you see for our congregants? How can all of us who are concerned participate with you in seeking this goal of social justice?

KING: Thank you very much for raising that because I do think that is a good note to end on, and I would hope that somehow we can get some real support, not only for the overall struggle, but for the immediate campaign ahead in the city of Washington.

Let me say that we have failed to say something to America enough. I'm very happy that the Kerner Commission had the courage to say it. However difficult it is to hear, however shocking it is to hear, we've got to face the fact that America is a racist country. We have got to face the fact that racism still occupies the throne of our nation. I don't think we will ultimately solve the problem of racial injustice until this is recognized, and until this is worked on.

Racism is the myth of an inferior race, of an inferior people, and I think religious institutions, more than any other institutions in society, must really deal with racism. Certainly we all have a responsibility—the federal government, the local governments, our educational institutions. But the religious community, being the chief moral guardian of the over-all community should really take the primary responsibility in dealing with this problem of racism, which is largely attitudinal.

So I see one specific job in the educational realm: destroying the myths and the half-truths that have constantly been disseminated about Negroes all over the country and which lead to many of these racist attitudes, getting rid once and for all of the notion of white supremacy.

I think also I might say, concerning the Washington campaign, that there is a need to interpret what we are about or will be about in Washington because the press has gone out of its way in many instances to misinterpret what we will be doing in Washington.

There is a need to interpret to all of those who worship in our congregations what poor people face in this nation, and to interpret the critical nature of the problem. We are dealing with the problem of poverty. We must be sure that the people of our country will see this as a matter of justice.

The next thing that I would like to mention is something very practical and yet we have to mention it if we are going to have movements. We are going to bring in the beginning about 3,000 people to Washington from fifteen various communities. They are going to be poor people, mainly unemployed people, some who are too old to work, some who are too young to work, some who are too physically disabled to work, some who are able to work but who can't get jobs. They are going to be coming to Washington to bring their problems, to bring their burdens to the seat of government, and to demand that the government do something about it.

Being poor, they certainly don't have any money. I was in Marks, Mississippi the other day and I found myself weeping before I knew it. I met boys and girls by the hundreds who didn't have any shoes to wear, who didn't have any food to eat in terms of three square meals a day, and I met their parents, many of whom don't even have jobs. But not only do they not have jobs, they are not even getting an income. Some of them aren't on any kind of welfare, and I literally cried when I heard men and women saying that they were unable to get any food to feed their children.

We decided that we are going to try to bring this whole community to Washington, from Marks, Mississippi. They don't have anything anyway. They don't have anything to lose. And we decided that we are going to try to bring them right up to Washington where we are going to have our Freedom School. There we are going to have all of the things that we have outlined and that we don't have time to go into now, but in order to bring them to Washington it is going to take money.

They'll have to be fed after they get to Washington, and we would hope that those who are so inclined, those who have a compassion for the least of these God's children, will aid us financially. Some will be walking and we'll be using church busses to get them from point to point. Some will be coming up on mule train. We're going to have a mule train coming from Mississippi, connecting with Alabama, Georgia, going right on up, and in order to carry that out you can see that financial aid will be greatly needed.

But not only that. We need bodies to bring about the pressure that I have mentioned to get Congress and the nation moving in the right direction. The stronger the number, the greater this movement will be.

We will need some people working in supportive roles, lobbying in Washington, talking with the Congressmen, talking with the various departments of government, and we will need some to march with us as we demonstrate in the city of Washington. Some have already done this, like Rabbi Gendler and others. When we first met him it was in Albany, Georgia and there, along with other rabbis and Protestant clergymen and Catholic clergymen, we developed a movement. And there have been others—as I said earlier, Rabbi Heschel in Selma and other movements.

The more of this kind of participation that we can get, the more helpful it will be, for after we get the 3,000 people in Washington, we want the non-poor to come in in a supportive role. Then on June fifteenth we want to have a massive march on Washington. You see, the 3,000 are going to stay in Washington at least sixty days, or however long we feel it is necessary, but we want to provide an opportunity once more for thousands, hundreds of thousands of people to come to Washington, reminiscent of March 1963 when thousands of people said we are here because we endorse the demands of the poor people who have been here all of these weeks trying to get Congress to move. We would hope that as many people in your congregations as you can find will come to Washington on June fifteenth.

You can see that it is a tremendous logistics problem and it means real organization, which we are getting into. We would hope that all of our friends will go out of their way to make that a big day, indeed the largest march that has ever taken place in the city of Washington.

These are some of the things that can be done. I'm sure I've missed some, but these are the ones that are on my mind right now and I believe that this kind of support would bring new hope to those who are now in very despairing conditions. I still believe that with this kind of coalition of conscience we will be able to get something moving again in America, something that is so desperately needed.

GENDLER: I think that all of us, Dr. King, recall the words of Professor Heschel at the beginning of this evening. He spoke of the word, the vision, and the way that you provide. We certainly have heard words of eloquence, words which at the same time were very much to the point, and through these I think we have the opportunity now to share more fully in your vision.

As for the way, it is eminently clear that the paths you tread are peaceful ones leading to greater peace. You may be sure that not only have we heard your words and not only do we share your vision, but many of us will take advantage of the privilege of accompanying you in further steps on the path that all of us must tread. Thank you, Dr. King.

REV. DR. MARTIN LUTHER KING, JR., was born in Atlanta, Georgia, in 1929. He went to Morehouse College at age fifteen and, after graduating with a BA in sociology, went to seminary school in Pennsylvania, then earned a PhD in theology from Boston University. Appointed pastor of the Dexter Avenue Baptist Church in Montgomery, Alabama, in 1954, he shortly thereafter became leader of the 1955 Montgomery bus boycott organized after the arrest of Rosa Parks, a black woman who refused to move to the back of the bus. He went on to become one of the founders of the Southern Christian Leadership Conference; deliver his famous "I Have a Dream" speech at the March on Washington in 1963; and play crucial roles in the Selma Voting Rights Movement, the Chicago Freedom Movement, opposition to the Vietnam War, and the Poor People's campaign, among many other major humanitarian efforts. King was assassinated on April 4, 1968, in Memphis, Tennessee. The Civil Rights Act of 1968 was passed by Congress one week later, on April 11.

RICHARD D. HEFFNER was the host and creator of *The Open Mind*, a current-affairs talk show that began broadcasting on public television in 1956. He is best remembered for his 1952 book *A Documentary History of the United States*. He also coauthored the book *Conversations with Elie Wiesel*, with the Nobel laureate. He died in 2013.

JULIUS WATIES WARING was a federal judge and is today remembered for his outspoken stance that segregation was unconstitutional, and his dissenting opinions that made possible the U.S. Supreme Court's 1954 *Brown v. Board of Education* decision. From 1942 to 1952, he served as a federal judge assigned to the U.S. District Court in Charleston, South Carolina. He died in 1968.

MIKE WALLACE was a pioneering American journalist, best known for his fifty years of reporting on *60 Minutes*, for which he earned a Lifetime Achievement Emmy in 2003. Before *60 Minutes*, he was host of a popular interview program on local New York television, *Night Beat*. He died in 2012.

ROBERT PENN WARREN was a poet, novelist, and one of the founders of the school of literary criticism known as New Criticism. His novel *All the King's Men* won the Pulitzer Prize in 1946. He also won the Pulitzer Prize for poetry in 1958, and again in 1979. He is the only writer to win in two categories. He published a collection of interviews with prominent civil rights leaders—*Who Speaks for the Negro?*—in 1965. He died in 1989.

ABRAHAM JOSHUA HESCHEL was a major twentieth-century Jewish theologian and philosopher. He participated in the Selma Civil Rights Marches with King, among other demonstrations. He died in 1972.

RABBI EVERETT GENDLER has been described as "the father of Jewish environmentalism." He has also been closely associated with causes such as the Jewish Nonviolence and Civil Rights Movements.

THE LAST INTERVIEW SERIES

KURT VONNEGUT: THE LAST INTERVIEW

"I think it can be tremendously refreshing if a creator of literature has something on his mind other than the history of literature so far. Literature should not disappear up its own asshole, so to speak."

$15.95 / $17.95 CAN
978-1-61219-090-7
ebook: 978-1-61219-091-4

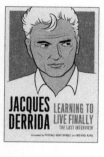

LEARNING TO LIVE FINALLY: THE LAST INTERVIEW
JACQUES DERRIDA

"I am at war with myself, it's true, you couldn't possibly know to what extent . . . I say contradictory things that are, we might say, in real tension; they are what construct me, make me live, and will make me die."

translated by PASCAL-ANNE BRAULT and MICHAEL NAAS

$15.95 / $17.95 CAN
978-1-61219-094-5
ebook: 978-1-61219-032-7

ROBERTO BOLAÑO: THE LAST INTERVIEW

"Posthumous: It sounds like the name of a Roman gladiator, an unconquered gladiator. At least that's what poor Posthumous would like to believe. It gives him courage."

translated by SYBIL PEREZ and others

$15.95 / $17.95 CAN
978-1-61219-095-2
ebook: 978-1-61219-033-4

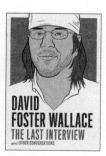

DAVID FOSTER WALLACE: THE LAST INTERVIEW

"I don't know what you're thinking or what it's like inside you and you don't know what it's like inside me. In fiction . . . we can leap over that wall itself in a certain way."

$15.95 / $15.95 CAN
978-1-61219-206-2
ebook: 978-1-61219-207-9

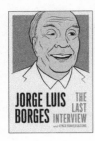

JORGE LUIS BORGES: THE LAST INTERVIEW

"Believe me: the benefits of blindness have been greatly exaggerated. If I could see, I would never leave the house, I'd stay indoors reading the many books that surround me."

translated by KIT MAUDE

$15.95 / $15.95 CAN
978-1-61219-204-8
ebook: 978-1-61219-205-5

HANNAH ARENDT: THE LAST INTERVIEW

"There are no dangerous thoughts for the simple reason that thinking itself is such a dangerous enterprise."

$15.95 / $15.95 CAN
978-1-61219-311-3
ebook: 978-1-61219-312-0

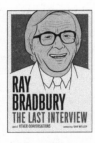

RAY BRADBURY: THE LAST INTERVIEW

"You don't have to destroy books to destroy a culture. Just get people to stop reading them."

$15.95 / $15.95 CAN
978-1-61219-421-9
ebook: 978-1-61219-422-6

JAMES BALDWIN: THE LAST INTERVIEW

"You don't realize that you're intelligent until it gets you into trouble."

$15.95 / $15.95 CAN
978-1-61219-400-4
ebook: 978-1-61219-401-1

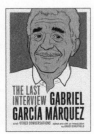

GABRIEL GÁRCIA MÁRQUEZ: THE LAST INTERVIEW

"The only thing the Nobel Prize is good for is not having to wait in line."

$15.95 / $15.95 CAN
978-1-61219-480-6
ebook: 978-1-61219-481-3

THE LAST INTERVIEW SERIES

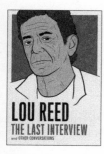

LOU REED: THE LAST INTERVIEW

"Hubert Selby. William Burroughs. Allen Ginsberg. Delmore Schwartz . . . I thought if you could do what those writers did and put it to drums and guitar, you'd have the greatest thing on earth."

$15.95 / $15.95 CAN
978-1-61219-478-3
ebook: 978-1-61219-479-0

ERNEST HEMINGWAY: THE LAST INTERVIEW

"The most essential gift for a good writer is a built-in, shockproof, shit detector."

$15.95 / $20.95 CAN
978-1-61219-522-3
ebook: 978-1-61219-523-0

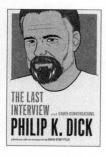

PHILIP K. DICK: THE LAST INTERVIEW

"The basic thing is, how frightened are you of chaos? And how happy are you with order?"

$15.95 / $20.95 CAN
978-1-61219-526-1
ebook: 978-1-61219-527-8

NORA EPHRON: THE LAST INTERVIEW

"You better *make* them care about what you think. It had better be quirky or perverse or thoughtful enough so that you hit some chord in them. Otherwise, it doesn't work."

$15.95 / $20.95 CAN
978-1-61219-524-7
ebook: 978-1-61219-525-4

JANE JACOBS: THE LAST INTERVIEW

"I would like it to be understood that all our human economic achievements have been done by ordinary people, not by exceptionally educated people, or by elites, or by supernatural forces."

$15.95 / $20.95 CAN
978-1-61219-534-6
ebook: 978-1-61219-535-3

J. D. SALINGER: THE LAST INTERVIEW

"Q: Have you ever granted an interview to anyone?
A: Knowledgeably? No.
Q: Have you ever granted an interview unknowledgeably to anyone?
A: Apparently, yes."

$16.99 / $22.99 CAN
978-1-61219-589-6
ebook: 978-1-61219-590-2

DAVID BOWIE: THE LAST INTERVIEW

"I have no time for glamour. It seems a ridiculous thing to strive for . . . A clean pair of shoes should serve quite well enough."

$16.99 / $22.99 CAN
978-1-61219-575-9
ebook: 978-1-61219-576-6

OLIVER SACKS: THE LAST INTERVIEW

"So this was the story, and he wrote to me and said, *Can you understand? Can you help? What's happened?*"

$15.99 / $21.99 CAN
978-1-61219-577-3
ebook: 978-1-61219-578-0

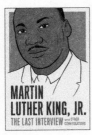

MARTIN LUTHER KING, JR.: THE LAST INTERVIEW

"Injustice anywhere is a threat to justice everywhere."

$15.99 / $21.99 CAN
978-1-61219-616-9
ebook: 978-1-61219-617-6